First World War
and Army of Occupation
War Diary
France, Belgium and Germany

19 DIVISION
58 Infantry Brigade
Welsh Regiment
9th Battalion
18 July 1915 - 31 March 1919

WO95/2092/2

The Naval & Military Press Ltd
www.nmarchive.com
Published in association with The National Archives

Published by

The Naval & Military Press Ltd

Unit 10 Ridgewood Industrial Park,

Uckfield, East Sussex,

TN22 5QE England

Tel: +44 (0) 1825 749494

www.naval-military-press.com

www.nmarchive.com

This diary has been reprinted in facsimile from the original. Any imperfections are inevitably reproduced and the quality may fall short of modern type and cartographic standards.

© **Crown Copyright**
Images reproduced by permission of The National Archives, London, England, 2015.

Contents

Document type	Place/Title	Date From	Date To
Heading	2092/2 9th Bn Welsh Regiment		
Heading	19th Division 58th Infy Bde 9th Bn Welsh Regt Jly 1915-Mar 1919		
Heading	9th Battn The Welsh Regiment. July To September (18.7.15 To 30.9.15) 1915		
War Diary	Southampton	18/07/1915	18/07/1915
War Diary	Havre	19/07/1915	20/07/1915
War Diary	Neille Les Ardres	21/07/1915	22/07/1915
War Diary	Arques	23/07/1915	23/07/1915
War Diary	Norrent Fontes	24/07/1915	30/07/1915
War Diary	Haverskerque	31/07/1915	04/08/1915
War Diary	Calonne-Sur-Lys	05/08/1915	05/08/1915
War Diary	Calonne	06/08/1915	16/08/1915
War Diary	Calonne & Pont Du Hem	17/08/1915	18/08/1915
War Diary	Pont Du Hem	19/08/1915	26/08/1915
War Diary	Calonne	27/08/1915	28/08/1915
War Diary	Croix Marmuse	29/08/1915	29/08/1915
War Diary	Reserve Sub-Section Ind I.A.	30/08/1915	03/09/1915
War Diary	Sub Section Ind IA	04/09/1915	26/09/1915
War Diary	Reserve Sub Section Ind IA	27/09/1915	28/09/1915
War Diary	Le Touret	29/09/1915	29/09/1915
War Diary	Pont Fixe & Cuinchy	30/09/1915	30/09/1915
War Diary	Pont Fixe	30/09/1915	30/09/1915
Heading	58th Inf. Bde. 19th Div. 9th Battn. The Welch Regiment. October 1915		
War Diary	Pont Fixe & Cuinchy	01/10/1915	06/10/1915
War Diary	Pont Fixe & Cuinchy To Paradis	07/10/1915	07/10/1915
War Diary	Paradis	08/10/1915	13/10/1915
War Diary	Paradis To Les Lobes	14/10/1915	14/10/1915
War Diary	Les Lobes	15/10/1915	23/10/1915
War Diary	Les Lobes To Sub Section Ind II B	24/10/1915	24/10/1915
War Diary	Sub Section Ind II B	25/10/1915	30/10/1915
War Diary	Sub Section Ind II B To Reserve Le Touret	31/10/1915	31/10/1915
Heading	58th Inf. Bde. 19th Div. 9th Battn. The Welch Regiment. November 1915		
Heading	War Diary Of The 9th Battalion Welsh Regt From The 1st November 1915 To The 30th November 1915		
Map			
War Diary	Le Touret	01/11/1915	07/11/1915
War Diary	Ind II B	08/11/1915	12/11/1915
War Diary	Le Touret	13/11/1915	17/11/1915
War Diary	Les Lobes	18/11/1915	23/11/1915
War Diary	Lesart	24/11/1915	30/11/1915
Heading	58th Inf. Bde. 19th Div. 9th Battn. The Welch Regiment. December 1915		
Heading	War Diary 9th (Service) Bn The Welch Regt Period Month Of December 1915		
War Diary	Le Sart (near Merville)	01/12/1915	02/12/1915
War Diary	Lesart To Trenches	03/12/1915	03/12/1915
War Diary	Trenches	04/12/1915	06/12/1915

War Diary	Trenches to Reserve Billets	07/12/1915	07/12/1915
War Diary	Reserve Billets Richebourg St Vaast	08/12/1915	10/12/1915
War Diary	Reserve Billets Bout Deville 8 Maisons & Croix Barbee	11/12/1915	11/12/1915
War Diary	Reserve Billets Bout Deville 8 Maisons & Croix Barbee Reserve Billets	12/12/1915	12/12/1915
War Diary	Reserve Billets To Les Lobes	13/12/1915	13/12/1915
War Diary	Les Lobes	14/12/1915	18/12/1915
War Diary	Les Lobes To Trenches	19/12/1915	19/12/1915
War Diary	Trenches	20/12/1915	22/12/1915
War Diary	Trenches To Bde Reserve	23/12/1915	23/12/1915
War Diary	Bde Reserve Croix Barbee	24/12/1915	26/12/1915
War Diary	Reserve Billets Croix Barbee To Trenches	27/12/1915	27/12/1915
War Diary	Trenches	28/12/1915	30/12/1915
War Diary	Trenches To Bde Reserve Croix Barbee	31/12/1915	31/12/1915
Heading	9th Welch Rgt. Vol 5 Jany 1916		
Heading	War Diary 9th (Ser) Bn. The Welch Regt. January 1916		
War Diary	Croix Barbee	01/01/1916	03/01/1916
War Diary	Croix Barbee To Les Lobes	04/01/1916	04/01/1916
War Diary	Les Lobes	05/01/1916	18/01/1916
War Diary	King's Rd	19/01/1916	22/01/1916
War Diary	King's Rd To Merville	23/01/1916	23/01/1916
War Diary	Merville	24/01/1916	31/01/1916
Heading	9th (Service) Battn The Welch Regiment The Diary February 1916		
War Diary	Merville	01/02/1916	13/02/1916
War Diary	Merville To La Gorgue	14/02/1916	14/02/1916
War Diary	La Gorgue	15/02/1916	15/02/1916
War Diary	La Gorgue To Trenches	16/02/1916	16/02/1916
War Diary	Trenches	17/02/1916	17/02/1916
War Diary	Trenches To Pont Du Hem	18/02/1916	18/02/1916
War Diary	Pont Du Hem	19/02/1916	19/02/1916
War Diary	Pont Du Hem To Trenches	20/02/1916	20/02/1916
War Diary	Trenches	20/02/1916	21/02/1916
War Diary	Trenches To Pont Du Hem	22/02/1916	22/02/1916
War Diary	Pont Du Hem	23/02/1916	23/02/1916
War Diary	Pont Du Hem To Robermetz	24/02/1916	24/02/1916
War Diary	Robermetz	25/02/1916	29/02/1916
Heading	War Diary 9th Battalion The Welch Regt March 1916 Vol 7		
War Diary	Robermetz	01/03/1916	01/03/1916
War Diary	Kings Road	02/03/1916	04/03/1916
War Diary	Rue Du Bois	05/03/1916	07/03/1916
War Diary	Les Lobes	08/03/1916	12/03/1916
War Diary	Croix Barbee	13/03/1916	13/03/1916
War Diary	Neuve Chappelle	14/03/1916	17/03/1916
War Diary	Croix Barbee	18/03/1916	21/03/1916
War Diary	Neuve Chapelle	22/03/1916	23/03/1916
War Diary	La Gorgue	24/03/1916	25/03/1916
War Diary	Rue Du Bois	26/03/1916	27/03/1916
War Diary	Kings Road	28/03/1916	31/03/1916
Heading	9th Battn Welch Regiment War Diary April 1916		
War Diary	Ferme Du Bois	01/04/1916	04/04/1916
War Diary	Kings Road	05/04/1916	08/04/1916
War Diary	Ferme Du Bois	09/04/1916	12/04/1916
War Diary	Kings Road	13/04/1916	16/04/1916
War Diary	Ferme Du Bois	17/04/1916	19/04/1916

War Diary	Belle Chapelle	20/04/1916	20/04/1916
War Diary	Robecq	21/04/1916	22/04/1916
War Diary	Erny St Julien	23/04/1916	30/04/1916
Heading	War Diary 9th (Service) Battn The Welch Regt May 1916 Vol 9		
War Diary	Erny-St Julien	01/05/1916	06/05/1916
War Diary	Erny-St Julien To Berguette	07/05/1916	07/05/1916
War Diary	Longeau To Flesselles	08/05/1916	08/05/1916
War Diary	Flesselles	09/05/1916	19/05/1916
War Diary	Flesselles To Roman Camp	20/05/1916	20/05/1916
War Diary	Roman Camp	21/05/1916	21/05/1916
War Diary	Roman Camp To Flesselles	22/05/1916	22/05/1916
War Diary	Flesselles	23/05/1916	28/05/1916
War Diary	Flesselles To Gorenflos	29/05/1916	29/05/1916
War Diary	Gorenflos To Neuilly L'Hopital	30/05/1916	30/05/1916
War Diary	Neuilly L'Hopital	30/05/1916	31/05/1916
Heading	9th Bn The Welsh Regt War Diary June 1916 Vol 10		
War Diary	Neuilly L'Hopital	01/06/1916	09/06/1916
War Diary	Neuilly L'Hopital To Gorenflos	10/06/1916	10/06/1916
War Diary	Gorenflos to Flesseles	11/06/1916	11/06/1916
War Diary	Flesselles to Frechencourt	12/06/1916	12/06/1916
War Diary	Frechencourt to Albert Camp	13/06/1916	18/06/1916
War Diary	Albert Camp	19/06/1916	30/06/1916
War Diary	Albert Camp To Preliminary Trenches		
Heading	58th Inf. Bde. 19th Div. 9th Battn. The Welch Regiment. July 1916		
Heading	War Diary 9th (Ser) Battn The Welch Regt July 1916 Vol 11		
War Diary	Albert To Usna Tara Line	01/07/1916	01/07/1916
War Diary	Usna Tara Line	02/07/1916	03/07/1916
War Diary	X20A 0.5 To X20 B 4.3	04/07/1916	05/07/1916
War Diary	Tara-Usna Line	06/07/1916	06/07/1916
War Diary	Heligoland	07/07/1916	07/07/1916
War Diary	X15d 0.0.	08/07/1916	09/07/1916
War Diary	Baizeux Wood	10/07/1916	21/07/1916
War Diary	Mametz Wood	21/07/1916	23/07/1916
War Diary	Bazentin Le Petit	23/07/1916	29/07/1916
War Diary	Becourt Wood	29/07/1916	30/07/1916
War Diary	Bethencourt	30/07/1916	30/07/1916
Heading	58th Brigade. 19th Division. 1/9th Battalion The Welch Regiment August 1916 Vol 12		
Heading	9th Service Battalion The Welch Regiment War Diary August 1916 Vol 12		
War Diary	Behencourt	01/08/1916	03/08/1916
War Diary	Pont Remy	04/08/1916	06/08/1916
War Diary	Bailleul	07/08/1916	07/08/1916
War Diary	R.C. Farm	08/08/1916	19/08/1916
War Diary	Butterfly Camp	20/08/1916	25/08/1916
War Diary	Rossignol	26/08/1916	31/08/1916
Heading	9th Ser Batt The Welch Regiment War Diary September 1916 Vol 13		
War Diary	R.C. Farm	01/09/1916	03/09/1916
War Diary	Locke	04/09/1916	04/09/1916
War Diary	Nieppe	05/09/1916	08/09/1916
War Diary	Surrey HQ Farm	08/09/1916	13/09/1916
War Diary	Chappelle	14/09/1916	14/09/1916

War Diary	Rompue	15/09/1916	20/09/1916
War Diary	Outersteene	21/09/1916	30/09/1916
Heading	9th (Ser) Battn The Welch Regiment War Diary October 1916 Vol 14		
War Diary	Outersteene	01/10/1916	05/10/1916
War Diary	Doullens	06/10/1916	06/10/1916
War Diary	Warnimont	07/10/1916	07/10/1916
War Diary	Hebuterne	08/10/1916	16/10/1916
War Diary	Vauchelles	17/10/1916	17/10/1916
War Diary	Herisart	18/10/1916	21/10/1916
War Diary	Bouzincourt	22/10/1916	22/10/1916
War Diary	Reserve Camp	23/10/1916	30/10/1916
Heading	9th (Ser) Bn The Welch Regiment War Diary November 1916 Vol 15		
War Diary	Donnetts Post Bulgar Trench	01/11/1916	05/11/1916
War Diary	Wood Post	06/11/1916	11/11/1916
War Diary	X 2.a.	12/11/1916	12/11/1916
War Diary	Staff Redoubt	13/11/1916	17/11/1916
War Diary	X 2a.	18/11/1916	18/11/1916
War Diary	Wellington Huts	19/11/1916	19/11/1916
War Diary	Staff Redoubt	20/11/1916	22/11/1916
War Diary	Wellington Huts	23/11/1916	23/11/1916
War Diary	Warloy	24/11/1916	24/11/1916
War Diary	Doullens	25/11/1916	25/11/1916
War Diary	Heuzecourt	26/11/1916	30/11/1916
Heading	9th (Ser) Battalion. The Welch Regiment War Diary December 1916 Vol 16		
War Diary	Heuzecourt	01/12/1916	31/12/1916
Heading	9th (Ser) Battalion The Welch Regiment War Diary January 1917 Vol 17		
War Diary	Heuzecourt	01/01/1917	28/01/1917
War Diary	The Line	29/01/1917	31/01/1917
Heading	War Diary 9th (Service) Battalion The Welch Regiment February 1917 Vol 18		
War Diary	Sailly Au Bois	01/02/1917	01/02/1917
War Diary	The Line	04/02/1917	04/02/1917
War Diary	Courcelles	09/02/1917	09/02/1917
War Diary	Coigneux	10/02/1917	10/02/1917
War Diary	Bus-En Artois	19/02/1917	19/02/1917
War Diary	Courcelles	27/02/1917	27/02/1917
War Diary	The Line	28/02/1917	28/02/1917
Heading	9th Service Battalion The Welch Regiment War Diary March 1917 Vol 19		
War Diary	The Line	01/03/1917	31/03/1917
Heading	9th (Ser) Battalion The Welch Regiment War Diary April 1917 Vol 20		
War Diary	Line	04/04/1917	19/04/1917
War Diary	Berthen	24/04/1917	30/04/1917
Heading	9th (Ser) Battalion The Welch Regiment War Diary May 1917 Vol 21		
War Diary	Line	01/05/1917	26/05/1917
Heading	9th (Ser) Battalion The Welch Regiment War Diary June 1917 Vol 22		
War Diary		03/06/1917	30/06/1917
Heading	9th (Ser) Battalion The Welch Regiment War Diary July 1917 Vol 23		

War Diary		02/07/1917	30/07/1917
War Diary	The Line	01/08/1917	02/08/1917
War Diary	Irish House	03/08/1917	05/08/1917
War Diary	Bailleul	07/08/1917	07/08/1917
War Diary	Bayenghem	10/08/1917	10/08/1917
War Diary	Frontier Camp	27/08/1917	27/08/1917
Heading	War Diary Sept 1917 9 Welch Regt. Vol 25		
War Diary		01/09/1917	29/09/1917
Operation(al) Order(s)	Operation Orders. No. 25 By Lieut-Colonel W. Godfrey D.S.O. Comdg. 9th Battn. Welch Regt. Appendix I	19/07/1917	19/07/1917
Operation(al) Order(s)	Operation Order By Lieut-Colonel W. Godfrey D.S.O. Comdg. 9th Battalion Welch Regiment.	17/09/1917	17/09/1917
Miscellaneous	Contact Patrols.	17/09/1917	17/09/1917
Miscellaneous	Administrative Orders. By Lieut Colonel W. Godfrey. D.S.O. Comdg 9th Battalion Welch Regt.	17/09/1917	17/09/1917
Miscellaneous	Amendment To Operation Orders. By Lieut Colonel W. Godfrey. D.S.O. Comdg 9th Battn Welch Regiment.	19/09/1917	19/09/1917
Map			
Miscellaneous			
Heading	9th (S) Bn. The Welch Regiment War Diary October 1917 Vol 26		
War Diary		01/10/1917	30/11/1917
Miscellaneous	Headquarters, 58th Brigade	31/12/1917	31/12/1917
Heading	9th (S) Bn The Welch Regt War Diary December 1917 Vol 28		
War Diary		23/12/1917	31/12/1917
Heading	9th (Service) Bn The Welch Regt War Diary January 1918 Vol 29		
War Diary	Ribecourt	01/01/1918	31/01/1918
Heading	9th (S) Bn The Welch Regt February 1918 Vol 30		
War Diary	In The Field	01/02/1918	28/02/1918
Heading	19th Division 58th Brigade 9th Battalion The Welch Regiment March 1918		
Heading	9th (S) Bn The Welch Regt March 1918 Vol 31		
War Diary		01/03/1918	31/03/1918
Miscellaneous	Headquarters 58th Inf Bde.	03/04/1918	03/04/1918
Miscellaneous	9th Batt The Welch Regt	02/04/1918	02/04/1918
Heading	58th Brigade 19th Division 1/9th Battalion The Welch Regiment April 1918		
War Diary	Locre	01/04/1918	30/04/1918
Miscellaneous	58th Infantry Bde	24/04/1918	24/04/1918
Miscellaneous	9th (S) Bn The Welch Regiment	24/04/1918	24/04/1918
War Diary	In The Line	01/05/1918	10/05/1918
War Diary	Camp	11/05/1918	12/05/1918
War Diary	Wylder	13/05/1918	17/05/1918
War Diary	St Germain Le Ville	18/05/1918	28/05/1918
Miscellaneous	9th (S) Bn The Welch Regiment.	15/06/1918	15/06/1918
War Diary	Line	01/06/1918	19/06/1918
War Diary	Hautvillers	20/06/1918	20/06/1918
War Diary	Crammont	21/06/1918	21/06/1918
War Diary	Broussy Le Grand	22/06/1918	30/06/1918
War Diary	Vassemont	01/07/1918	01/07/1918
War Diary	Sommesous	02/07/1918	02/07/1918
War Diary	Anvin	03/07/1918	03/07/1918
War Diary	Coupelle Veille	04/07/1918	04/07/1918
War Diary	Ledingham	05/07/1918	11/07/1918

War Diary	Rely	12/07/1918	06/08/1918
War Diary	Support Line	07/08/1918	10/08/1918
War Diary	Front Line	11/08/1918	14/08/1918
War Diary	Chocques	15/08/1918	18/08/1918
War Diary	Support Line	19/08/1918	23/08/1918
War Diary	Front Line	24/08/1918	31/08/1918
Miscellaneous	58th The Brigade Headquarters	06/10/1918	06/10/1918
War Diary		01/09/1918	03/09/1918
War Diary	Locon	05/09/1918	10/09/1918
War Diary	Front Line	11/09/1918	14/09/1918
War Diary	Line of Retention.	15/09/1918	18/09/1918
War Diary	Front Line	19/09/1918	22/09/1918
War Diary	Locon	23/09/1918	27/09/1918
War Diary	Line	28/09/1918	30/09/1918
Heading	9th (Service) Bn The Welch Regt October 1918 Vol 38		
War Diary	Line	01/10/1918	01/10/1918
War Diary	Pressy-Les-Pernes	02/10/1918	04/10/1918
War Diary	Barly	05/10/1918	07/10/1918
War Diary	Cantaing	08/10/1918	10/10/1918
War Diary	Cagnoncles	12/10/1918	12/10/1918
War Diary	Rieux	16/10/1918	22/10/1918
Operation(al) Order(s)	58th Infantry Brigade Order No. 277 Appendix 1	10/10/1918	10/10/1918
Operation(al) Order(s)	Operation Orders No. 16 By Lieut Col. H.L. Jones. D.S.O. Comdg 9th (S) Bn The Welch Regiment. Appendix 2	19/10/1918	19/10/1918
Heading	9th (S) Bn The Welch Regiment November 1918 Vol 39		
War Diary	Rieux	01/11/1918	01/11/1918
War Diary	Haussy	02/11/1918	02/11/1918
War Diary	Vendegies	02/11/1918	03/11/1918
War Diary	L'Ermitage near Aulnois	10/11/1918	29/11/1918
Miscellaneous	Appendix A		
Miscellaneous	Administrative Orders By Lieut Colonel W. Godfrey. D.S.O. Comdg 9th Battn Welch Regt. Appendix "A"		
Miscellaneous	Operation Orders By Lieut Colonel W. Godfrey. D.S.O. Comdg 9th Battn Welch Regt		
Miscellaneous	Administrative Orders By Lieut Colonel W. Godfrey. D.S.O. Comdg 9th Battn Welch Regt.		
Operation(al) Order(s)	Operation Orders No. 21 By Major L. Hammill. D.S.O. M.C. Comdg 9th (S) Bn The Welch Regiment. Appendix "B"	02/11/1918	02/11/1918
Miscellaneous	A Form Messages And Signals.		
Operation(al) Order(s)	58th Infy. Bde. Order No. 285 Appendix D		
Miscellaneous	Addendum No. 2 to 58th Bde. Order No. 285	03/11/1918	03/11/1918
Operation(al) Order(s)	57th Infantry Brigade Order No. 258 Appendix E	07/11/1918	07/11/1918
Operation(al) Order(s)	57th Infantry Brigade Order No. 259 Appendix F	08/11/1918	08/11/1918
Heading	9th (S) Bn The Welch Regt. December 1918 Vol 40		
War Diary	Halloy-Les Pernois	01/12/1918	10/12/1918
War Diary	Berteaucourt	11/12/1918	31/12/1918
Heading	9th (S) Bn The Welch Regiment January 1919 Vol 41		
War Diary	Berteaucourt	01/01/1919	31/01/1919
Heading	9th (S) Bn The Welch Regt February 1919 Vol 42		
War Diary	Berteaucourt	01/02/1919	23/02/1919
War Diary	Villers L'Hopital	24/02/1919	28/02/1919
Miscellaneous	9th (S) The Welch Regt March 1919 Vol 43		
War Diary	Villers L'Hopital	07/03/1919	31/03/1919

2092/2

9TH Bn
WELSH REGIMENT

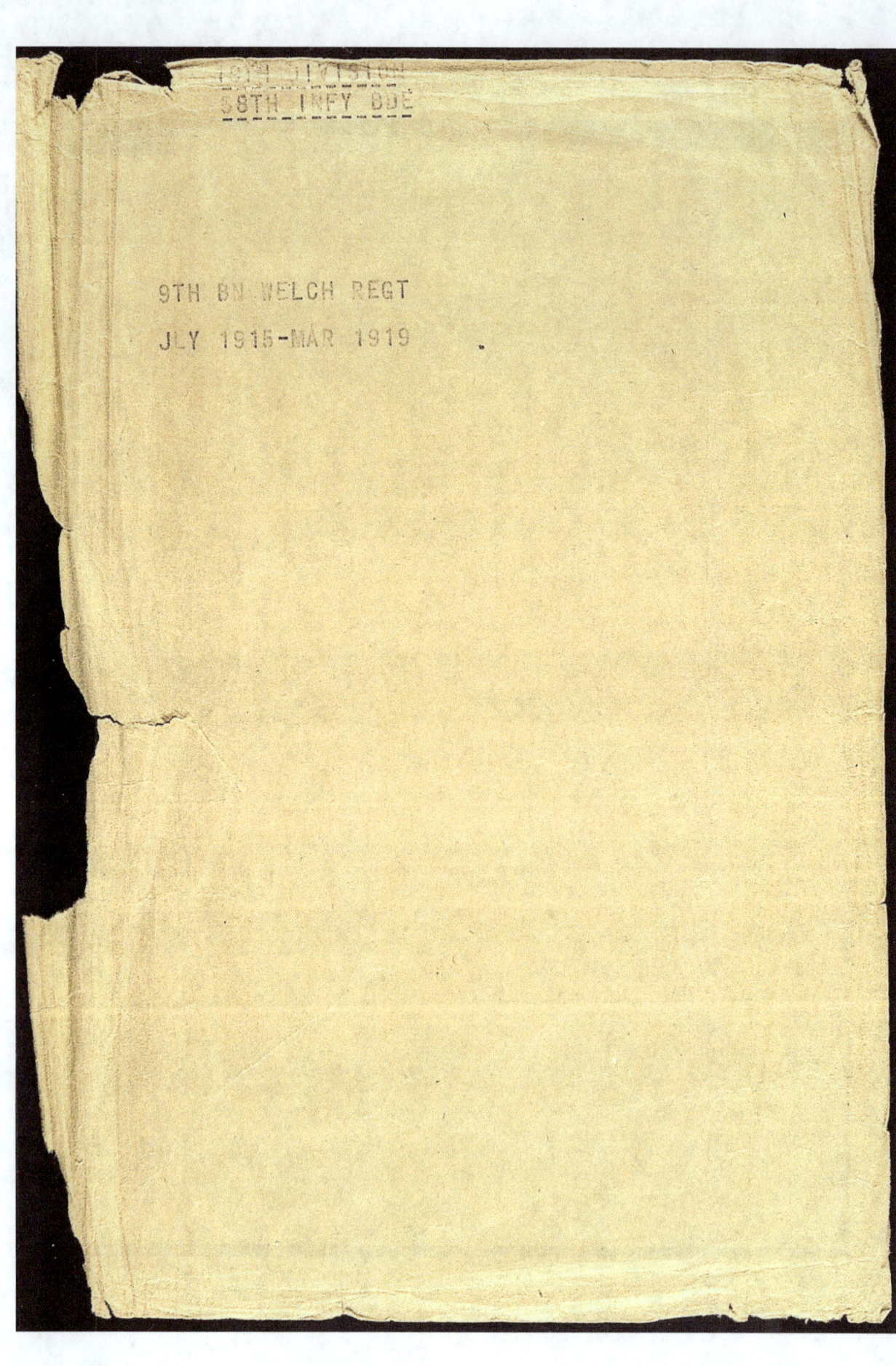

19TH DIVISION
58TH INFY BDE

9TH BN WELCH REGT
JLY 1915-MAR 1919

58th Inf.Bde.
19th Div.

Battn. disembarked
Havre from England
19.7.15.

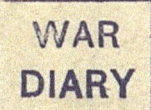

9th BATTN. THE WELCH REGIMENT.

JULY to SEPTEMBER

(18.7.15 to 30.9.15)

1915

WAR DIARY or INTELLIGENCE SUMMARY

Army Form C. 2118

July to September 1915

9th (Ser.) Bn The Welsh Regiment

(Erase heading not required.)

Instructions regarding War Diaries and Intelligence Summaries are contained in F.S. Regs., Part II. and the Staff Manual respectively. Title Pages will be prepared in manuscript.

Place	Date	Hour	Summary of Events and Information	Remarks and references to Appendices
SOUTHAMPTON	19/7/15		The Battalion embarked on H.M. Transport MONAS QUEEN.	
HAVRE	19/7/15	3:30 A	The Battalion arrived at HAVRE, disembarked and proceeded to No1 REST CAMP ST ADRESSE.	
HAVRE	20/7/15	10.50 P	The Battalion entrained at POINT No 4.	
NEILLE LES ARDRES	21/7/15		The Battalion arrived ARDUICQ near MONTESOLIER, BUCHY, ABBEVILLE, BOULOGNE, and CALAIS and proceeded to billets at NEILLE LES ARDRES.	
NEILLE LES ARDRES	22/7/15		The Battalion remained in their billets.	
ARQUES	23/7/15		The Battalion marched from NEILLE LES ARDRES to ARQUES and occupied billets there.	
NORRENT-FONTES	24/7/15		The Battalion marched from ARQUES to NORRENT-FONTES.	
NORRENT-FONTES	25/7/15		The Battalion remained in billets.	
NORRENT-FONTES	26/7/15		The Battalion remained in billets.	
NORRENT-FONTES	27/7/15		The Battalion remained in billets.	

WAR DIARY
or
INTELLIGENCE SUMMARY

(Erase heading not required.)

Army Form C. 2118

Instructions regarding War Diaries and Intelligence Summaries are contained in F.S. Regs., Part II. and the Staff Manual respectively. Title Pages will be prepared in manuscript.

Place	Date	Hour	Summary of Events and Information	Remarks and references to Appendices
NORRENT-FONTES.	28/7/15		The Battalion went for a route march and returned to their billets.	
NORRENT-FONTES.	29/7/15		The Battalion went for a route march and returned to their billets.	
NORRENT-FONTES.	30/7/15		The Battalion went for a route march and returned to their billets.	
HAVERSKERQUE	31/7/15		The Battalion marched from NORRENT-FONTES via ST-VENANT to HAVERSKERQUE.	
HAVERSKERQUE	1/8/15		The Battalion remained in billets.	
HAVERSKERQUE	2/8/15		The Battalion remained in billets.	
HAVERSKERQUE	3/8/15		The Battalion remained in billets.	
HAVERSKERQUE	4/8/15		The Battalion remained in billets.	
CALONNE SUR-LYS	5/8/15		The Battalion marched from HAVERSKERQUE to CALONNE-SUR-LYS and went into billets.	
CALONNE	6/8/15		The Battalion remained in billets.	
CALONNE	7/8/15		The Battalion went for a route march and returned to billets.	
CALONNE	8/8/15		The Battalion remained in billets.	
CALONNE	9/8/15		The Battalion remained in billets.	
CALONNE	10/8/15		The Battalion remained in billets.	
CALONNE	11/8/15		The Battalion went for a Brigade route march and returned to their billets.	

WAR DIARY
or
INTELLIGENCE SUMMARY
(Erase heading not required.)

Army Form C. 2118

Instructions regarding War Diaries and Intelligence Summaries are contained in F. S. Regs., Part II. and the Staff Manual respectively. Title Pages will be prepared in manuscript.

Place	Date	Hour	Summary of Events and Information	Remarks and references to Appendices
CALONNE	12/8/15		The Battalion remained in billets.	
CALONNE	13/8/15		Night march 9.20pm 13th to 2.20am 14th & return of Billets	
DO.	14/8/15		The Battalion remained in billets	
DO	15/8/15			
DO	16/8/15		The Battalion practised the occupation of defensive posts in the PONT-DU-VILLE area & returned to billets.	
CALONNE & PONT DU HEM	17/8/15		A Coy moved to LA BASSEE road near PONT DU HEM and took over billets. Other Coy. attached to DEHRA DUN BDE. for instruction in trench duties	
CALONNE & PONT DUHEM	18/8/15		B Coy moved to LA BASSEE road as for A Coy above. Two platoons of A Coy & Machine Gun Trench went into trenches with 1/4 Gurkha Rifles.	
PONT DUHEM	19/8/15		Bn HQ and C & D Coys moved to LA BASSEE road & took over billets as for A & B Coys above.	
PONT DU HEM	20/8/15		Two platoons of A Coy relieved party in trenches	
DO	21/8/15		Two platoons in trenches. Remainder in billets	
DO	22/8/15		Two platoons and grenadier platoon relieve two platoons in trenches	
DO	23/8/15		Two platoons in trenches. Remainder in billets	
DO	24/8/15		D Company relieve party in trenches	
DO	25/8/15		D Company in trenches. Remainder in billets	
DO	26/8/15		D Company relieved. Battalion. No relief.	
CALONNE	27/8/15		Bn. marched from PONT DU HEM to CALONNE SUR LYS and went into billets.	

WAR DIARY
or
INTELLIGENCE SUMMARY
(Erase heading not required.)

Army Form C. 2118

Instructions regarding War Diaries and Intelligence Summaries are contained in F.S. Regs., Part II. and the Staff Manual respectively. Title Pages will be prepared in manuscript.

Place	Date	Hour	Summary of Events and Information	Remarks and references to Appendices
CALONNE	28/8/15		In billets.	
CROIX MARMUSE	29/8/15		The Battn marched from CALONNE to CROIX MARMUSE & went into billets. Grenadier platoon & Machine Gun. Service & Reserve Sections attached to Brigade Headquarters.	
Reserve Sub-sector IND IA.	30/8/15		The Battn moved via GORRE wood to Reserve at ESTAMINET corner (Reserve IND I.A.) relieving 2nd BORDER REGT. 1 off joined Battn. 40 N.C.O.s & men. Distribution in Reserve Line. A & B Coys in INTERMEDIATE Line. D Company in FESTUBERT, C Coy behind INTERMEDIATE line.	
Do	31/8/15		Battn in Reserve as above.	
Do	1/9/15		do	
Do	2/9/15		do	
Do	3/9/15		do	
Sub-section IND IA	4/9/15		The Battn relieved 9/Cheshire Regt in trenches Subsection IND IA, Relief completed 11.15 am. 15th inst. Disposition. Front line A Coy on right, B Coy on left. In support trenches C Coy. In reserve trenches D Coy.	
Do	5/9/15		do	
Do	6/9/15		do	
Do	7/9/15		do. Casualties 3	
Do	8/9/15		do. Casualties 3	
Do	9/9/15		do. Casualties 1	
Do	10/9/15		do. Casualties 2	

WAR DIARY
or
INTELLIGENCE SUMMARY

(Erase heading not required.)

Army Form C. 2118

Place	Date	Hour	Summary of Events and Information	Remarks and references to Appendices
Sub section IND 1A	11.9.15		In Trenches Sub Section IND 1 A. Casualties 3	
do	12.9.15		Company relief placing D Coy right front, C Coy left front, B Coy in support & A Coy in Reserve. Casualties nil.	
do	13.9.15		Casualties nil	
do	14.9.15		Casualties 1	
do	15.9.15		Casualties 3	
do	16.9.15		Casualties 1 (Grenadier b Caton)	
do	17.9.15		Casualties 2	
do	18.9.15		Casualties nil	
do	19.9.15		Casualties nil	
do	20.9.15		The Batt. closed in to its right so as to have its left on FIFE ROAD (No. 4 Communication Trench). Company relief placing A 70 right front, B Co left front, C Co support & D Co Reserve i.e. in the original formation. The 9/RW Fusiliers closed in so as to bring its right to rest on FIFE ROAD (No. 4 Comm. Trench), and having the OB 4th Brigade on its left. The 9th Cheshire Regt moved back to the INTERMEDIATE line and the 6th Wiltshire moved to the North of 9th Wilts. in support of i.e. 9th Cheshire now in support of 9th Welsh., & 6th Wiltshire in support of 9th Royal Welsh Fusiliers.	

WAR DIARY
or
INTELLIGENCE SUMMARY

Army Form C. 2118

Instructions regarding War Diaries and Intelligence Summaries are contained in F.S. Regs., Part II. and the Staff Manual respectively. Title Pages will be prepared in manuscript.

(Erase heading not required.)

Place	Date	Hour	Summary of Events and Information	Remarks and references to Appendices
Sub Sector IND 1A	21.9.15		Bombardment of German line commenced. Casualties 3	
Do	22.9.15		Bombardment continued	
Do	23.9.15		Bombardment continued	
Do	24.9.15	4 am	Final arrangements made re attack. Bn HQ moved to front line P.22em About 4 am front line took up position for attack and C & D companies commenced moving up No 6 & No 4 communication trenches in readiness to support advanced companies. About 5.30 am orders received that gas	
Do	25.9.15	5.57am	attack would commence 5.50am. Smoke helmets put on. At 5.57am gas and smoke let off from cylinders & smoke candles. About 6.30 am a sheaf of coloured rockets was sent up from Regmt Headquarters (signal for attack to commence). Leading platoons, two from A Co & two	
		6.30am	from B Co, advanced over the parapet followed by supporting platoons of their companies. These were followed by leading platoons of C & D companies. Immediately Gas & smoke was observed. The enemy commenced a heavy bombardment with H.E. shells and swept the ground & parapet with rifle & machine gun fire. We still kept caught D Coy who by 6.30 am were in the new support trench & caused them heavy casualties. The leading and supporting platoons	
		6.40am	as soon as they were over the parapet were met by the most intense rifle & machine gun fire and suffered heavy casualties in that ground. By about	

WAR DIARY or INTELLIGENCE SUMMARY

(Erase heading not required.)

Army Form C. 2118

Place	Date	Hour	Summary of Events and Information	Remarks and references to Appendices
Sub Section MD 1A	26/9/15	6.45 am	The Casualties were already well over two hundred, and all outside the parapet were exposed to a deadly fire from the enemy machine gun & rifle fire, as no progress could be made the men were carried down the line, that the advance should stop, what those outside should endeavour to regain our parapet before it about 7am the unwounded men commenced to come back either through the gaps or over the parapet and from this time until midday the Battalion was being reformed and the 9th Cheshire Regt manned the parapet in case of counter attack.	
		12 am	Battalion relieved by O.T.R. to withdraw & dugout reserve trenches	
		1 pm		
		3.30 pm	Move completed about 3.30 pm	
Reserve do.	27/9/15	7am	In Reserve trenches. Work of carrying down dead & collecting rifles, kits etc carried on throughout the day. Intend to move back to INTERMEDIATE Line. Move completed about 6 pm. Parties at work catering equipment etc from the trenches.	
		12 nn	Batta. in INTERMEDIATE Line.	
do	28/9/15		Batta. in INTERMEDIATE LINE.	
LE TOURET	29/9/15		Relieved by 10th Royal Warwickshire Regt & moved back to billets at LE TOURET. Move completed about 9 pm.	
PONT FIXE & CUINCHY	30/9/15	12 noon	Marched to ready house 2. Epone with Btn. A.D.S.S. Marched off 2. Epone via GORRE, & LE QUESNOY to support at	

Army Form C. 2118

WAR DIARY
or
INTELLIGENCE SUMMARY

(Erase heading not required.)

Instructions regarding War Diaries and Intelligence Summaries are contained in F. S. Regs., Part II. and the Staff Manual respectively. Title Pages will be prepared in manuscript.

Place	Date	Hour	Summary of Events and Information	Remarks and references to Appendices
PONT FIXE	30/9/15	(continued)	PONT FIXE just S of LA BASSEE CANAL taking over support billets from 1/King's (Liverpool) Regiment. B Company found 100 men for garrison CUINCHY. Bn. HQ a remainder of Batln about PONT FIXE in Brewery & surrounding houses.	

C H Young Lt. Col.
Comndg 9 West Riding

1875 Wt. W593/826 1,000,000 4/15 J.B.C. & A. A.D.S.S./Forms/C. 2118.

58th Inf.Bde.
19th Div.

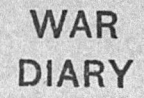

9th BATTN. THE WELCH REGIMENT.

OCTOBER

1915

WAR DIARY
or
INTELLIGENCE SUMMARY

(Erase heading not required.)

Army Form C. 2118

October 1915
9th (Ser) Bn. The Welsh Regt.

Instructions regarding War Diaries and Intelligence Summaries are contained in F. S. Regs., Part II. and the Staff Manual respectively. Title Pages will be prepared in manuscript.

Place	Date	Hour	Summary of Events and Information	Remarks and references to Appendices
PONT FIXE & CUINCHY	1.10.15		Battn. in support	
do	2.10.15		do. Carrying parties all day carrying cylinders to front line. Enemy shelled PONT FIXE & vicinity for two hours. About noon damaging bridge. Casualties 2.	
do	3.10.15	1 am	Report received that Germans had exploded mine in lines held by 6th WILTSHIRE REGT causing big gap in parapet. Working party of 85 sent up to repair damage. Remainder of day. Parties at work carrying cylinders to front line	
do	4.10.15		Carrying parties at work as above	
do	5.10.15		do	
do	6.10.15		do	
PONT FIXE & CUINCHY & PARADIS	7.10.15		Relived by 1st S. Staffordshire Regt. Moved back via Canal bank, G. FARRE, LE HAMEL & EGLISE to Reserve billets at PARADIS	
PARADIS	8.10.15		In reserve billets. Draft of 6 officers & 62 other ranks arrived at night.	
do	9.10.15		In reserve billets	
do	10.10.15		do	
do	11.10.15		do	
do	12.10.15		do	
do	13.10.15		do	

Army Form C. 2118

WAR DIARY
or
INTELLIGENCE SUMMARY
(Erase heading not required.)

Instructions regarding War Diaries and Intelligence Summaries are contained in F. S. Regs., Part II. and the Staff Manual respectively. Title Pages will be prepared in manuscript.

Place	Date	Hour	Summary of Events and Information	Remarks and references to Appendices
PARADIS to LES LOBES	14.10.15	4 p.m.	Batt. in Reserve billets. Moved to front billets at LES LOBES in the afternoon. Move complete 4 p.m.	
LES LOBES	15.10.15		In reserve billets LES LOBES	
do	16.10.15		do	
do	17.10.15		do	
do	18.10.15		do	
do	19.10.15		do	
do	20.10.15		do	
do	21.10.15		do	
do	22.10.15		do	
do	23.10.15		do	
LES LOBES to sub section IND II B	24.10.15 4.45 p.m. 9.30 p.m.		Batt. marched from Reserve billets LES LOBES, and took over front trenches sub section IND II B from 4th East Lancashire Regt. Relief completed 9.30 p.m.	
sub section IND II B	25.10.15		In trenches sub section IND II B. Front line right to left. D Coy, C Coy, B Coy. Reserve trenches A Coy. Also finding garrisons for MINROW, RYDE MARSDEN, and TUBE STATION POSTS.	
do	26.10.15		do	
do	27.10.15		do	

1875 Wt. W593/826 1,000,000 4/15 J.B.C. & A. A.D.S.S./Forms/C. 2118.

WAR DIARY
or
INTELLIGENCE SUMMARY

(Erase heading not required.)

Army Form C. 2118

Instructions regarding War Diaries and Intelligence Summaries are contained in F. S. Regs, Part II. and the Staff Manual respectively. Title Pages will be prepared in manuscript.

Place	Date	Hour	Summary of Events and Information	Remarks and references to Appendices
Sub section IND II B	28.10.15		In trenches. Sub section IND II B.	
do	29.10.15		do	
do	30.10.15		do	
Sub section IND II B to Reserve LE TOURET	31.10.15		Batt. relieved by 6th WILTSHIRE REGT and went into Reserve at LE TOURET with A Coy in RUE DE L'EPINETTE and B Coy in RUE DES CHAVATTES.	

C.H. Fairy Lt Col
Comdg 3rd Wilts Regt
4-11-15

58th Inf.Bde.
19th Div.

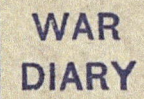

9th BATTN. THE WELCH REGIMENT.

NOVEMBER

1915

WAR DIARY
or
INTELLIGENCE SUMMARY.

Army Form C. 2118

War Diary
of the
9th Battalion Welch Regt
from the
1st November 1915. to the 30th November 1915.

BELGIUM AND PA...

1/20,000

WAR DIARY
INTELLIGENCE SUMMARY
(Erase heading not required.)

Army Form C. 2118

9th Batln Welsh Regt

Place	Date	Hour	Summary of Events and Information	Remarks and references to Appendices
LE TOURET	1/11/15		In Reserve, Headquarters and C and D Companies were in Billets at LE TOURET, B Coy on RUE DES CHAVATTES and A Coy on RUE DE L'ÉPINETTE.	
Do	2/11/15		In Reserve as above, Working parties were supplied daily.	
Do	3/11/15			
Do	4/11/15			
Do	5/11/15		fire - work - on front line - and support trenches	
Do	6/11/15			
Do	7/11/15		The Battalion relieved the 6th Battalion Wiltshire Regiment in Sub-Section IND II B. A Coy were on the left, B Coy in the centre, C Coy on the right and D Coy in reserve and furnished the garrisons for Keeps.	
IND II B	8/11/15		Occupied Sub-Section IND II B as above	
Do	9/11/15		Do	
Do	10/11/15		Do	
Do	11/11/15		Do	

WAR DIARY or **INTELLIGENCE SUMMARY**

Army Form C. 2118

9th Battalion Welsh Regt

(Erase heading not required.)

Place	Date	Hour	Summary of Events and Information	Remarks and references to Appendices
IND II B.	12/11/15		The Battalion was relieved in sub-section IND II B. by the 6" Bn Wiltshire Regiment. Relief completed 7.30 p.m. Battalion went into Reserve with Batn Headquarters and A and C Coys about LE TOURET B. Coy in RUE DES CHAVATTES and D Coy in RUE DE L'EPINETTE.	
LE TOURET	13/11/15		In Reserve Billets at LE TOURET.	
Do	14/11/15		In Reserve Billets as above. Working parties were furnished daily for work on front line and support trenches.	
Do	15/11/15			
Do	16/11/15			
LE TOURET	17/11/15		The Battalion moved back into Divisional Reserve and occupied billets at LES LOBES.	
LES LOBES	18/11/15		In Divisional Reserve Billets.	
Do	19/11/15			
Do	20/11/15			
Do	21/11/15		In Divisional Reserve Billets. Lt-Col Young and Sergeant Renwal proceeded on leave to England.	

Army Form C. 2118

9th Battalion Welsh Regt

WAR DIARY
or
INTELLIGENCE SUMMARY
(Erase heading not required.)

Instructions regarding War Diaries and Intelligence Summaries are contained in F. S. Regs., Part II. and the Staff Manual respectively. Title Pages will be prepared in manuscript.

Place	Date	Hour	Summary of Events and Information	Remarks and references to Appendices
LES LOBES	22/11/15		In Divisional Reserve.	
LES LOBES	23/11/15		The Battalion moved back into Corps Reserve and occupied hutts near LESART on the MERVILLE – HAVERSKERQUE Road.	
LESART	24/11/15		Rest billets as above.	
Do	25/11/15		Rest billets as above.	
Do	26/11/15		Rest billets as above. Working party of 300 men proceeded by motor-buses to billets half way between ROUGE-CROIX and PONT DU HEM for works on drainage behind line held by GUARDS DIVISION. 100 men at this work by night.	
Do	28/11/15		Rest billets as above. Party of 200 men worked on the drainage system by day and 100 men by night.	
Do	29/11/15		In Rest billets as above. The party of 300 men reported to Battalion.	
Do	30/11/15		In Rest billets as above.	

J. D. Crofts Lieut Col
Comdg 9th Bn Welsh Regt.

58th Inf.Bde.
19th Div.

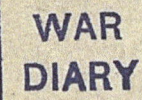

9th BATTN. THE WELCH REGIMENT.

DECEMBER

1915

Army Form C. 2118

WAR DIARY
or
INTELLIGENCE SUMMARY
(Erase heading not required.)

War Diary
9th (Service) Bn The Welch Regt
Period
Month of December 1915

Army Form C. 2118

WAR DIARY
or
INTELLIGENCE SUMMARY
(Erase heading not required.)

Instructions regarding War Diaries and Intelligence Summaries are contained in F.S. Regs., Part II. and the Staff Manual respectively. Title Pages will be prepared in manuscript.

Place	Date	Hour	Summary of Events and Information	Remarks and references to Appendices
LE SART (near MERVILLE)	December 1st		Battalion in Corps Rest.	
do	2nd		do.	
LE SART to Richebourg	3rd	9.30am	Battalion moved from Rest Billets & crossed via MERVILLE, PARADIS, NEUVE CHAPPELLE & LACOUTURE to RICHEBOURG ST. VAAST. Men rested and dinners were served. Battalion relieved the 5th Bn. Sherwood Foresters (146 Brim T.F.) and the Left Company of the 8th Bn. Leicestershire Regt. (146 Brim T.F.) in the Right Subsection Right sector of Northern Division of XI Corps front. (extent from FARM CORNER on right to COPSE STREET inclusive Battn HQ at EDWARD ROAD	
		6.30pm	S.9.A.6.6½) Relief completed 8.30pm. on night	
Trenches	4th		In Trenches as above	
do	5th		do	
do	6th		do	
Trenches to Reserve billets	7th	10.30pm	Battalion was relieved by 9th Bn. Cheshire Regt. & moved to Brigade Reserve Billets at RICHEBOURG ST. VAAST. Relief completed 10.30pm. Battalion occupied following posts. RICHEBOURG ST. VAAST, EDWARD, HENS, ARGYLE, GROTTO, BOYES, RAGS, HUNTER, and SCOTT.	

1875 Wt. W593/826 1,000,000 4/15 J.B.C. & A. A.D.S.S./Forms/C. 2118.

WAR DIARY
or
INTELLIGENCE SUMMARY
(Erase heading not required.)

Army Form C. 2118

Instructions regarding War Diaries and Intelligence Summaries are contained in F.S. Regs., Part II. and the Staff Manual respectively. Title Pages will be prepared in manuscript.

Place	Date	Hour	Summary of Events and Information	Remarks and references to Appendices
Reserve Billets RICHEBOURG ST VAAST	8th		In Reserve billets as above	
do	9th		do	
do	10th		do	
do to BOUT DEVILLE & MAISONS & CROIX BARBEE	11th		The Battalion was relieved by the 10th Battn. Warwickshire Regt and marched back to Brigade Reserve at BOUT DEVILLE, MAISONS & CROIX BARBEE.	
do. Reserve Billets	12th		In reserve billets as above	
do. LES LOBES	13th	9.15am	Battalion moved out of billets at 9.45am and proceeded to the LES LOBES - LACON billeting area. in Divisional Reserve	
LES LOBES	14th		In Divisional Reserve LES LOBES - LACON.	
do	15th		do	
do	16th		Lieut Col. Cooke from 5th Bn South Wales Borderers took over Command of the Battalion vice Lieut Col. C.H. Young returned to England	

WAR DIARY
or
INTELLIGENCE SUMMARY
(Erase heading not required.)

Army Form C. 2118

Instructions regarding War Diaries and Intelligence Summaries are contained in F. S. Regs., Part II. and the Staff Manual respectively. Title Pages will be prepared in manuscript.

Place	Date	Hour	Summary of Events and Information	Remarks and references to Appendices
LES LOBES	17th		In Divisional Reserve as above	
do	18th		do	
LES LOBES 19th to Trenches	19th		Battalion moved out of billets early in the afternoon and took over LEFT SECTOR, RIGHT SUB-SECTION, RIGHT DIVISION of XIth CORPS Line from 7th Bn. East Lancashire Regt. (relief from COPSE STREET on right (inclusive) to LA BASSÉE ROAD (inclusive) on left) Bn HQ RUE DU BOIS S.10.A.6.35.	
Trenches	20th		In Trenches as above	
do	21st		do	
do	22nd		do	
do to Res Reserve	23rd		Battalion relieved in Trenches by 6th Bn The Wiltshire Regiment and moved back to Brigade Reserve at CROIX BARBÉE and along road towards LACOUTURE. Following posts occupied. LAN'S DU N.E. LORETTO, ST. VAAST, RUE DU PUITS, CROIX BARBÉE, PENIN MARRIAGE.	
Bde Reserve CROIX BARBÉE	24th		In Brigade Reserve as above	
do	25th		do	
do	26th		do	

WAR DIARY
or
INTELLIGENCE SUMMARY
(Erase heading not required.)

Army Form C. 2118

Instructions regarding War Diaries and Intelligence Summaries are contained in F.S. Regs., Part II. and the Staff Manual respectively. Title Pages will be prepared in manuscript.

Place	Date	Hour	Summary of Events and Information	Remarks and references to Appendices
Reserve billets CROIX BARBEE to trenches	27th		Battalion moved into trenches relieving 6th Batn. the Wiltshire Regiment in former line.	
trenches	28th		As trenches as above) More artillery activity noticeable on part of the Enemy. Trenches & RUE DO BOIS shelled continually.	
trenches	29th		do	
trenches	30th		do	
trenches to Bat Reserve CROIX BARBEE	31st		Relieved by 6th Bn. Wiltshire Regt. Battalion moved back to Brigade Reserve billets at CROIX BARBEE occupying LANSDOWNE, LORETTO, ST YMAST posts & forming Permanent Caretaking Guard from Regiment in RUE DU PUITS post.	

J.S. Crosby Lieut. Col.
Comdg 9th Bn. The Wilts Regiment.

9th Welch Rgt.
Vol: 5
Jany 1916

19th Div

Army Form C. 2118

WAR DIARY
or
INTELLIGENCE SUMMARY
(Erase heading not required.)

War Diary

9th (Ser) Bn: The Welch Regt.

January 1916.

WAR DIARY or INTELLIGENCE SUMMARY

Army Form C. 2118

(Erase heading not required.)

Instructions regarding War Diaries and Intelligence Summaries are contained in F. S. Regs., Part II. and the Staff Manual respectively. Title Pages will be prepared in manuscript.

Place	Date	Hour	Summary of Events and Information	Remarks and references to Appendices
CROIX BARBEE	1-1-16		Battn. in Brigade Reserve for portion of line between COPSE STREET and the LA BASSEE ROAD.	
do	2-1-16		do	
do	3-1-16		do	
do	4-1-16	11 a.m.	Brigade relief. 58th. Bde. relieved by 57th. Bde. Battn. relieved by 6th. Bn. North Staffordshire	
to		-3 p.m.	Regiment & moved back to Divisional Reserve at LES LOBES – LOCON. Battn: H.Q.	
LES LOBES.			LOCON. 3 Companies on road between LES LOBES & LOCON. 1 Company at LE TOMBE WILLOT.	
LES LOBES	5-1-16		Battn. in Divisional Reserve LES LOBES.	
do	6-1-16		do	
do	7-1-16		do	
do	8-1-16		do	
do	9-1-16		do	
do	10-1-16		At 5 p.m., two parties each of 2 Officers, 8 Grenadiers, and 12 bayonet men, with a supporting party of 2 Officers & 40 other ranks left billets & proceeded to Rest House No. 5. LORETTO ROAD. Rested these until 11 p.m. and proceeded into front line via COPSE STREET. Narrow wooden bridges three opposite COPSE STREET and three opposite MOLE STREET had been previously laid, by the supporting party, across the ditch running parallel to our front line. 2nd. Lieut. R. G. Cooke and 2 scouts went out at MOLE STREET, and 2 scouts at COPSE STREET to reconnoitre the German wire and report.	
		12 midnight		

Instructions regarding War Diaries and Intelligence Summaries are contained in F. S. Regs., Part II. and the Staff Manual respectively. Title Pages will be prepared in manuscript.

WAR DIARY or INTELLIGENCE SUMMARY

(Erase heading not required.)

Army Form C. 2118

Place	Date	Hour	Summary of Events and Information	Remarks and references to Appendices
	11-1-16	2-50 a.m. 3-15 a.m.	The COPSE STREET patrol returned. The MOLE STREET patrol returned and reported that there were strong German working parties in their wire which was well cut at points 5.10.C.9.5. & 3.10.D.7.9.	
		3-45 a.m.	Acting on this the two bombing parties went out and advanced to the German wire. The right (on COPSE STREET) party. (2nd Lieut. J.H. Loree and D.L. Davies) reached the German wire when 2nd Lieut. Davies' men threw four grenades into the German trench and 2nd Lieut. Loree's party threw three on to their parapet. The party was bombed in return and retired without casualties.	
		4-15 a.m.	The left (on MOLE STREET) party. (Capt. A.H. Thomas and 2nd Lieut. B.H. Bourne) reached the German wire and threw about 8 grenades into a working party on the wire. These took effect and the working party retired to their own parapet. Heavy rifle fire was opened on our party which then retired without loss.	
		6-30 a.m. 8 a.m.	The parties were collected and returned at once to the Rest house and from thence to Reserve billets.	
LES LOBES	11-1-16		Battn in Divisional Reserve. LES LOBES - LOCON.	
do	12-1-16		do	
do	13-1-16		do	
do	14-1-16	3-30 p.m.	Battn started moving and took over Right Section Right Subsector from part of 14th & part of 10th Bn: Royal Welsh Fusiliers. Disposition:-	
			Front line RUE DE CAILLOUX to FARM CORNER - - - 1 Company. FARM CORNER - - - - 40 men.	

WAR DIARY
or
INTELLIGENCE SUMMARY
(Erase heading not required.)

Army Form C. 2118

Instructions regarding War Diaries and Intelligence Summaries are contained in F.S. Regs., Part II. and the Staff Manual respectively. Title Pages will be prepared in manuscript.

Place	Date	Hour	Summary of Events and Information	Remarks and references to Appendices
			Support Posts TUBE STATION & vicinity — — — 1 Company.	
			CHOCOLATE }	
			DEAD COW }	
			"Z" ORCHARD } — — — — 1 Company	
			ALBERT }	
			DOGS. }	
			Reserve Bullets WHISKY CORNER	
			& POST TEETOTAL CORNER — — — 1 Company	
			Grenadiers.	
			Bn. H.Q. ALBERT ROAD.	
	15-1-16		In trenches as above	
	16-1-16		do	
	17-1-16		do	
	18-1-16	1 a.m.	A party of 2 Officers, 10 Grenadiers, and 10 bayonet men as an advanced party, and 1 Officer, 6 Grenadiers, and 6 bayonet men as a covering party were told off to attack the German lines between S.16.A.6.1. and S.16.A.6.4. (North of FME COUR D'AVOUE).	
		3-40am	The covering party went out from Point S.16.A.0.1. and took up a position to guard the right & left flanks of the attacking party.	
		3-55am	The attacking party went out from the same point and passed through the covering party which were in a position facing outwards. The attacking party crawled about 200 yards towards the German wire. At about 20 yards from the German parapet they were held up by a ditch varying from 8 to 12 feet broad	

WAR DIARY
or
INTELLIGENCE SUMMARY
(Erase heading not required.)

Army Form C. 2118

Place	Date	Hour	Summary of Events and Information	Remarks and references to Appendices
			and about 2 yards from the German wire. A search was made for crossings but nothing passable could be found to right or left. Neither could any lanes be seen through the wire which seemed to consist of loose unsupported chevaux de frise. As it was found impossible to cross the ditch, and as no passages were found the party returned without having been seen by the enemy. A sentry was seen silhouetted against the parapet opposite, and there was smoke rising from a fire on his left. No talking or coughing was heard, no sounds of work were heard, and only three flares went up from this part of the line during the operations. It would appear from this that the trench was lightly held.	
		5 a.m.	Both parties returned without casualties.	
		4·30 p.m.	Bn: relieved by 6th. Bn. Wiltshire Regt in this subsection, but still kept garrison of 15 men and 2 bombers each, in ALBERT & "Z" Orchard POSTS.	
		8·30 p.m.	The Battn moved to Brigade Reserve billets in KING'S ROAD and RUE DU BOIS.	
KING'S RD.	19-1-16		Battn in Brigade Reserve as above.	
do	20-1-16		do Working parties varying from 100 to 200 men at work	
do	21-1-16		do each night either in front line or at New Breastwork	
do	22-1-16		do PRINCES ROAD. Also about WINDY CORNER	
do	23-1-16	1 p.m.	Divisional relief. Battn: by 14th. Battn. Royal Welch Fusiliers (38th Division) and marched
MERVILLE				

Army Form C. 2118

WAR DIARY
or
INTELLIGENCE SUMMARY
(Erase heading not required.)

Instructions regarding War Diaries and Intelligence Summaries are contained in F. S. Regs., Part II. and the Staff Manual respectively. Title Pages will be prepared in manuscript.

Place	Date	Hour	Summary of Events and Information	Remarks and references to Appendices
MERVILLE	24-1-16	6 p.m.	via LACOUTURE, VIEILLE CHAPELLE, PARADIS & MERVILLE, to Corps Reserve about 1 mile N.W. of MERVILLE.	
do	25-1-16		In Corps Reserve as above. Training commenced.	
do	26-1-16		In Corps Reserve as above.	
do	27-1-16		In Corps Reserve as above.	
do	28-1-16		In Corps Reserve as above. Training continued in Arms drill, Squad, Platoon and Company drill, bombing, sniping, signalling etc. Route marching.	
do	29-1-16			
do	30-1-16			
do	31-1-16			

J. F. Cooke Lieut-Col.
Comdg 9th Bn. The Welch Regiment.

Army Form C. 2118

VOL 6

WAR DIARY
or
INTELLIGENCE SUMMARY
(Erase heading not required.)

9th (Service) Batn
The Welch Regiment

War Diary
February 1916

Army Form C. 2118

WAR DIARY
or
INTELLIGENCE SUMMARY
(Erase heading not required.)

Instructions regarding War Diaries and Intelligence Summaries are contained in F.S. Regs., Part II. and the Staff Manual respectively. Title Pages will be prepared in manuscript.

Place	Date	Hour	Summary of Events and Information	Remarks and references to Appendices
MERVILLE	January 1		Battalion in Corps Reserve, billeted about one mile N.W. of MERVILLE.	
do	2			
do	3			
do	4			
do	5		In Corps Reserve as above. Training proceeded with	
do	6			
do	7			
do	8			
do	9			
do	10			
do	11			
do	12			
do	13			
MERVILLE to LA GORGUE	14	9 am 12 noon	Moved to LA GORGUE and took over billets in the town from Brigade Reserve 2nd Bn Grenadier Guards	
LA GORGUE	15		Battalion in Brigade Reserve as above	

1875 Wt. W593/826 1,000,000 4/15 J.B.C. & A. A.D.S.S./Forms/C. 2118.

Army Form C. 2118

WAR DIARY
or
INTELLIGENCE SUMMARY
(Erase heading not required.)

Instructions regarding War Diaries and Intelligence
Summaries are contained in F. S. Regs., Part II.
and the Staff Manual respectively. Title Pages
will be prepared in manuscript.

Place	Date	Hour	Summary of Events and Information	Remarks and references to Appendices
LA GORGUE to Trenches	16		Battalion moved into Trenches taking over left subsector left division from 2nd Worcest. Distribution from MOATED GRANGE (late NOPPH) to ERITH STREET. A Coy on the right, B in the centre, D on the left. C Coy in posts as follows:- WINCHESTER GRANTS DREADNOUGHT NORTH TILLELOY ERITH Batn HQ WINCHESTER HOUSE.	
TRENCHES	17		Battalion in line as above.	
TRENCHES to PONT DU HEM	18		Battalion relieved by 6th Battn WILTSHIRE REGT and moved to Bat Reserve billets about PONT DU HEM and LA FLINQUE POST	
PONT DU HEM	19		In Bde Reserve as above.	
PONT DU HEM to TRENCHES	20		Battalion took over left sub-sector from 6th WILTSHIRE REGT (Distribution)	

1875 Wt. W593/826 1,000,000 4/15 J.B.C. & A. A.D.S.S./Forms/C. 2118.

Army Form C. 2118

WAR DIARY
or
INTELLIGENCE SUMMARY
(Erase heading not required.)

Instructions regarding War Diaries and Intelligence Summaries are contained in F.S. Regs., Part II. and the Staff Manual respectively. Title Pages will be prepared in manuscript.

Place	Date	Hour	Summary of Events and Information	Remarks and references to Appendices
TRENCHES	20		Distribution. C Coy on right. B Coy in centre. D Coy on left. A Coy in posts as under:- WINCHESTER G'RANTS DREADNOUGHT NORTH TILLELOY ERITH. Bn. H.Q. WINCHESTER HOUSE. 3 Lewis guns in front line + 1 in DREADNOUGHT POST. Battalion in line as above.	
TRENCHES	21			
TRENCHES to PONT DU HEM.	22		Relieved by 6th Batln. The WILTSHIRE REGT and moved to Brigade Reserve about PONT DUHEM and LA FLINQUE POST.	
PONT DU HEM	23		In Bde. Reserve as above.	
PONT DU HEM to ROBERMETZ	24		57th Brigade relieved by 57th Brigade. Battalion relieved by 10th Battn. Royal Warwickshire Regiment and moved into Divisional Reserve at ROBERMETZ about one mile E. of NEUVILLE. Battn HQ at M 24 D Y 9.	

1875 Wt. W593/826 1,000,000 4/15 J.B.C. & A. A.D.S.S./Forms/C. 2118.

WAR DIARY
or
INTELLIGENCE SUMMARY

(Erase heading not required.)

Army Form C. 2118

Instructions regarding War Diaries and Intelligence Summaries are contained in F. S. Regs., Part II. and the Staff Manual respectively. Title Pages will be prepared in manuscript.

Place	Date	Hour	Summary of Events and Information	Remarks and references to Appendices
BERMETZ	25		In Divisional Reserve as above. Training proceeded with.	
do	26			
do	27		do.	
do	28			
do	29			

J.S. Cooper Lieut Col.
Comdg. 9th Cheshire Regt.

1875 Wt. W593/826 1,000,000 4/15 J.B.C. & A. A.D.S.S./Forms/C. 2118.

Army Form C. 2118

WAR DIARY
or
INTELLIGENCE SUMMARY
(Erase heading not required.)

9 Welsh Vol 7

W.O. T.L.
6 sheets

War Diary
9th Battalion The Welsh Regt.
March 1916

WAR DIARY
or
INTELLIGENCE SUMMARY
(Erase heading not required.)

Army Form C. 2118

Place	Date	Hour	Summary of Events and Information	Remarks and references to Appendices
ROBERMETZ	1/3/16		Battalion moved from Divisional Reserve to Brigade Reserve at KINGS ROAD with small garrisons in LE TOURET LE TOURET N.E. CHAVATTE SCOTT HUNTER and RUE L'EPINETTE N. POSTS.	
KINGS ROAD	2/3/16		In Brigade Reserve as above	
To	3/3/16			
KINGS ROAD	4/3/16		Relieved 6th WILTSHIRE BATTN in the line from QUINQUE RUE CROSSING to FARM CORNER. Distribution C Coy right front. A Coy left front. B Coy right reserve (TUBE STN) with garrisons in ROPE TEA+COY and TEETOTAL breastworks and 2 platoons in BOURNEVILLE breastworks with local controls at CHOCOLATE and TEETOTAL corners. Headquarters in RUE DU BOIS.	
RUE DU BOIS	5/3/16 6/3/16		In line as above.	
To	7/3/16		Relieved by 23rd MANCHESTER REGT and moved back to Divisional Reserve at LES LOBES and neighbourhood.	

WAR DIARY
or
INTELLIGENCE SUMMARY

(Erase heading not required.)

Army Form C. 2118

Instructions regarding War Diaries and Intelligence Summaries are contained in F. S. Regs., Part II. and the Staff Manual respectively. Title Pages will be prepared in manuscript.

Place	Date	Hour	Summary of Events and Information	Remarks and references to Appendices
LES LOBES	8/3/16			
Do	9/3/16		In Divisional Reserve as above.	
Do	10/3/16			
Do	11/3/16		A party of 5 officers and 53 rank and file were taken in wagons from LES LOBES to the RUE DE BOIS to make a raid on the enemy's trenches between the FERME COUR D'AVOUÉ and the FERME DE BOIS. 2/Lieut DL DAVIES and 4 scouts went out about 12.30 am on the 12th and out and through four rows of the enemy's wire suspecting object in depth. On the other side of the wire there were few feet of wrecks of virgin wire 20 feet broad & in front of big wire -- then a visible object immediately in front of the enemy's parapet. It was considered rash to advance without losing the advantage of surprise and it was decided to abandon the raid. The party sitting the wire were covered by a machine gun party under 2/Lieut GAPP. The wire was cut at 4.6 and 7M. The party returned about 4.0 am.	

WAR DIARY
or
INTELLIGENCE SUMMARY
(Erase heading not required.)

Army Form C. 2118

Place	Date	Hour	Summary of Events and Information	Remarks and references to Appendices
LES LOBES	12.3.16		Batln marched from Divisional Reserve to Brigade reserve at CROIX BARBEE and RUE DE PUITS.	
CROIX BARBEE	13.3.16		Relieved 7th EAST LANCASHIRE REGT in Right Sub-section NEUVE CHAPELLE Sector. Disposition C on right A in Centre D on the left (1 platoon in HILLS REDOUBT) B. Coy in Reserve with 1 platoon at LANSDOWNE and 1 platoon in PORT ARTHUR KEEP.	
NEUVE CHAPELLE	14.3.16		In line as above.	
Do	15.3.16			
Do	16.3.16			
Do	17.3.16		Relieved by 6th BATTN WILTSHIRE REGT. BATTN marched to Brigade Reserve at CROIX BARBEE and RUE DE PUITS.	
CROIX BARBEE	18.3.16		In Brigade Reserve as above.	
Do	19.3.16			
Do	20.3.16			
Do	21.3.16		Relieved 6th BATTN WILTSHIRE in RIGHT SUB-SECTION NEUVE CHAPELLE Sector. Disposition B. Coy on right A in Centre D on Left (1 platoon in HILLS REDOUBT) and C in Reserve with one platoon at LANSDOWNE and one in PORT ARTHUR Keep.	

WAR DIARY
or
INTELLIGENCE SUMMARY
(Erase heading not required.)

Army Form C. 2118

Instructions regarding War Diaries and Intelligence Summaries are contained in F. S. Regs., Part II. and the Staff Manual respectively. Title Pages will be prepared in manuscript.

Place	Date	Hour	Summary of Events and Information	Remarks and references to Appendices
NEUVE CHAPELLE	22.3.16		In line as above.	
DO.	23.3.16		Relieved by 7" KINGS OWN LANCASTER REGT. Battn moved into DIVISIONAL RESERVE at LA GORGUE.	
LA GORGUE	24.3.16		In Divisional Reserve as above.	
LA GORGUE	25.3.16		The Battn relieved the 18" LANCASHIRE FUSILIERS in the right SUB-SECTION of the FERME DU BOIS SECTION. Distribution B Coy right front line A. left front line D Coy. TUBE STATION and ROPE KEEP. DEAD COW and CADBURY POSTS. C Coy occupied the TEETOTAL and the BOURNVILLE BREASTWORKS. (2 platoons in each).	
RUE DU BOIS	26.3.16		In line as above.	
Do	27.3.16		Relieved by the 6" BATTN WILTSHIRE REGT and Battalion proceeded into Brigade Reserve at KINGS ROAD. A working party of 2 officers and 100 other ranks was furnished for work under the R.E.	
KINGS ROAD	28.3.16		In Brigade Reserve as above. Working parties of two officers and 200 other ranks were furnished for work under the R.E.	
Do	29.3.16		In Brigade Reserve as above. Working parties of two officers and 200 other ranks were furnished for work under the R.E.	

WAR DIARY
or
INTELLIGENCE SUMMARY
(Erase heading not required.)

Army Form C. 2118

Place	Date	Hour	Summary of Events and Information	Remarks and references to Appendices
KINGS ROAD	30-3-16		The Brigade Reserve as above. Working parties of 250 other ranks furnished for work under the R.E.	
Do	31-3-16		Relieved the 6th Battn WILTSHIRE REGT in Right Sub-Section FERME DU BOIS Section. Distribution D Coy in Right front line C Coy left front line A in TEETOTAL and BOURNVILLE Breastworks (2 platoons in each) B Coy in TUBE STATION and furnishing garrisons for ROPE HEAD COW and CADBURY POSTS.	
	3.4.16			

W. Godfrey Major
Commanding 6th Battn the Welsh Regt.

9th Welsh Reg
Army Form C. 2118.

XIX Vol 8

WAR DIARY
or
INTELLIGENCE SUMMARY.
(Erase heading not required.)

9th Battn Welsh Regiment

War Diary

April 1916

9th Battalion Welch Regt.

Army Form C. 2118.

WAR DIARY
or
INTELLIGENCE SUMMARY.
(Erase heading not required.)

Instructions regarding War Diaries and Intelligence Summaries are contained in F. S. Regs., Part II. and the Staff Manual respectively. Title pages will be prepared in manuscript.

Place	Date	Hour	Summary of Events and Information	Remarks and references to Appendices
FERME DU BOIS	1-4-16		In the line in RIGHT SUB-SECTION FERME DU BOIS SECTION. Distribution D. Coy Right front line C Coy Left front line A Coy in Old and New Breastworks and B. Coy in TUBE STATION.	
Do	2-4-16		In line as above.	
Do	3-4-16			
Do	4-4-16		Relieved by 6th Batln WILTSHIRE REGT and Battalion proceeded into Brigade Reserve at KINGS ROAD.	
KINGS ROAD	5-4-16		In Brigade Reserve as above.	
Do	6-4-16			
Do	7-4-16			
Do	8-4-16		Relieved 6th BATTN WILTSHIRE REGT in RIGHT SUB-SECTION FERME DU BOIS SECTION.	
FERME DU BOIS	9-4-16		In line as above.	
Do	10-4-16			
Do	11-4-16			
Do	12-4-16		Relieved by 6th BATTN WILTSHIRE REGT and Battalion proceeded into Brigade Reserve at KINGS ROAD.	

WAR DIARY
or
INTELLIGENCE SUMMARY.
(Erase heading not required.)

Army Form C. 2118.

Instructions regarding War Diaries and Intelligence Summaries are contained in F. S. Regs., Part II. and the Staff Manual respectively. Title pages will be prepared in manuscript.

Place	Date	Hour	Summary of Events and Information	Remarks and references to Appendices
KINGS ROAD	13.4.16		In Brigade Reserve as above.	
Do	14.4.16			
Do	15.4.16			
Do	16.4.16		Relieved 6th BATTN WILTSHIRE REGT in RIGHT SUB-SECTION FERME DU BOIS Section. Distribution II by Left front line C Coy, Right front line A Coy in OLD and NEW BREASTWORKS and B Coy in TUBE STATION, DEAD COW POST and ROPE KEEP.	
FERME DUBOIS	17.4.16		In line as above	
	18.4.16			
Do	19.4.16		Relieved by 17th BATTN SHERWOOD FORESTERS and Battalion proceeded into Divisional Reserve Billets at VIELLE CHAPELLE.	
VIELLE CHAPELLE	20.4.16		Battalion moved into Corps Reserve Billets at ROBECQ.	
ROBECQ	21.4.16		In Corps Reserve as above	
Do	22.4.16		Battalion moved into GHQ Reserve for training. Bn. Headquarters and C & D Coys occupied billets at ERNY-ST-JULIEN and A and B Coys occupied billets at CUHEM.	

WAR DIARY
or
INTELLIGENCE SUMMARY.

(Erase heading not required.)

Army Form C. 2118.

Instructions regarding War Diaries and Intelligence Summaries are contained in F. S. Regs., Part II. and the Staff Manual respectively. Title pages will be prepared in manuscript.

Place	Date	Hour	Summary of Events and Information	Remarks and references to Appendices
ERNY ST JULIEN	23.4.16		The Battalion carried out Platoon and Company training	
Do	24.4.16		in allotted portions of the 1st Army Manoeuvring Area.	
Do	25.4.16			
Do	26.4.16			
Do	27.4.16		Battalion training was carried out in allotted	
Do	28.4.16		portions of the 1st Army Manoeuvring Area.	
Do	29.4.16			
Do	30.4.16			

S.G. Brooke
Lieut. Colonel
Commdg. 9th Batln Welsh Regt

Army Form C. 2118

9 Welch Regt

Vol 9

(19)

WAR DIARY
or
INTELLIGENCE SUMMARY.

War Diary
9th (Service) Battn The Welch Regt.

May 1916

WAR DIARY
or
INTELLIGENCE SUMMARY.

(Erase heading not required.)

Army Form C. 2118.

Instructions regarding War Diaries and Intelligence Summaries are contained in F. S. Regs., Part II. and the Staff Manual respectively. Title pages will be prepared in manuscript.

Place	Date	Hour	Summary of Events and Information	Remarks and references to Appendices
ERNY-ST JULIEN	1-5-16		Battalion Training	
do	2-5-16		Brigade Training	
do	3-5-16		Brigade Training	
do	4-5-16		Divisional Training	
do	5-5-16		Divisional Training	
do	6-5-16		In G.H.Q. Reserve	
do	7-5-16	5pm	Battalion marched to BERGUETTE station and entrained about 11pm	
BERGUETTE	do			
LONGEAU	8-5-16	7am	Arrived LONGEAU station detrained & marched via AMIENS to billets	
		2pm	at FLESSELLES	
FLESSELLES	9-5-16		In G.H.Q reserve. Platoon & Company training on ground in vicinity	
do	10-5-16			
do	11-5-16			
do	12-5-16			
do	13-5-16			
do	14-5-16			

WAR DIARY or INTELLIGENCE SUMMARY.

Army Form C. 2118.

Place	Date	Hour	Summary of Events and Information	Remarks and references to Appendices
FLESSELLES	15.5.16		In B.H.Q. Reserve as above. Company & platoon training continued	
do	16.5.16			
do	17.5.16			
do	18.5.16			
do	19.5.16			
do	20.5.16	10 am	Battalion moved to ROMAN CAMP near BELLOY SUR SOMME.	
ROMAN CAMP		3 pm	Outpost operations	
ROMAN CAMP	21.5.16		Continuation of outpost scheme as above.	
ROMAN CAMP to FLESSELLES	22.5.16	4:30 am	Battalion returned to FLESSELLES & reoccupied former billets	
FLESSELLES	23.5.16	9 am	In B.H.Q. Reserve Training continued	
	24.5.16			
	25.5.16			
	26.5.16			
	27.5.16			
	28.5.16			

WAR DIARY
or
INTELLIGENCE SUMMARY.
(Erase heading not required.)

Army Form C. 2118.

Place	Date	Hour	Summary of Events and Information	Remarks and references to Appendices
FLESSELLES	29:5:16	7am	Brigade moved to GORENFLOS and vicinity	
GORENFLOS		12:30pm	Battalion occupied billets at GORENFLOS	
GORENFLOS	30:5:16	7am	Brigade moved to ST RIQUIER Training area.	
NEUILLY L'HOPITAL		11:30am	Battalion occupied billets at NEUILLY L'HOPITAL	
NEUILLY L'HOPITAL	30/5/16		In billets	
do	31/5/16		Battalion Training in ST RIQUIER area.	

[signature] Major
Comdg 9th Bn The Welch Regt.

9th Welsh Regt
Army Form C. 2118.

WAR DIARY
or
INTELLIGENCE SUMMARY.
(Erase heading not required.)

XIX   Vol 10   June

9th Bn. the Welch Regt
War Diary
June 1916

Army Form C. 2118.

WAR DIARY
or
INTELLIGENCE SUMMARY.
(Erase heading not required.)

Instructions regarding War Diaries and Intelligence Summaries are contained in F.S. Regs., Part II. and the Staff Manual respectively. Title pages will be prepared in manuscript.

Place	Date	Hour	Summary of Events and Information	Remarks and references to Appendices
Neuilly	1st			
L'Hôpital	2nd		The Battn took part in Brigade & Divisional training daily on the St Riquier training area near Abbeville.	
do	3rd			
do	4th			
do	5th			
do	6th			
do	7th			
do	8th			
do	9th			
Neuilly L'Hôpital to	10th	8 am	The Brigade marched from Neuilly L'Hôpital area to Gorenflos and	
Gorenflos		12.30pm	occupied billets therein.	
Gorenflos to	11th	8 am	The Battalion detached from the Brigade & marched to Flesselles	
Flesselles		1pm	occupying billets therein	
Flesselles to	12th	8 am	The Battalion marched from Flesselles to Freshencourt and	
Freshencourt		1pm	occupied billets therein.	

Army Form C. 2118.

WAR DIARY
or
INTELLIGENCE SUMMARY.
(Erase heading not required.)

Instructions regarding War Diaries and Intelligence Summaries are contained in F. S. Regs., Part II. and the Staff Manual respectively. Title pages will be prepared in manuscript.

Place	Date	Hour	Summary of Events and Information	Remarks and references to Appendices
Freshencourt to Acket Camp	13th	8am	The Battn marched from Frechencourt to Acket Camp taking over Bivouacs from the 7th Battn Kings Own. (Jameson Brigade) 56th Brigade.	
	14th	10/am		
	15th		During this period the Battn was chiefly employed in supplying working parties by night & day under the supervision of the 84th and 91st Field Companies R.E. The work done consisted chiefly in the preparation of :-	
	16th			
	17th			
	18th			
Acket Camp	19th		(A) The new Assembly Trenches on the "Tara-Usna" line north East of Acket, which crossed the Acket - Bapaume road about 1000 yards behind our old front line;	
	20th			
	21st			
	22nd		B The new preliminary trenches South West of Acket which run for a distance of about 850 yards on each side of the railway, being close & parallel to it.	
	23rd			
	24th			
	25th			
	26th			
	27th		(C) Digging & covering in trenches to hold cable & telephone wires in and around Acket	
	28th			
	29th			
	30th			

Army Form C. 2118.

WAR DIARY
or
INTELLIGENCE SUMMARY.
(Erase heading not required.)

Instructions regarding War Diaries and Intelligence Summaries are contained in F. S. Regs., Part II. and the Staff Manual respectively. Title pages will be prepared in manuscript.

Place	Date	Hour	Summary of Events and Information	Remarks and references to Appendices
Albert Camp to Preliminary trenches			The Battn moved from bivouac about 9.0pm & formed up in the preliminary trenches S.W. of Albert referred to above. First line transport proceeded to bivouac about 800 yards west of Dernancourt.	

J H Cooke Lieut. Col.
9th Battn. The Welsh Regt.

VOL II

58th Inf.Bde.
19th Div.

WAR DIARY

9th BATTN. THE WELCH REGIMENT.

J U L Y

1 9 1 6

Vol II

9 Welsh Regt

War Diary.
9th (Sv) Batt. The Welsh Regt
July 1916.

WAR DIARY or INTELLIGENCE SUMMARY

Army Form C. 2118

865.

Place	Date	Hour	Summary of Events and Information	Remarks and references to Appendices
ALBERT to USNA - TARA LINE	July 1st	9pm	The Battn moved from preliminary trenches near the railway about ½ mile S.W. of ALBERT and proceeded by platoons through ALBERT & by OWEN communication trench running alongside the ALBERT - BAPAUME road to the USNA - TARA assembly trenches NE of ALBERT, which cross the ALBERT - BAPAUNE ROAD about 1000 yards behind our old front line. The whole of the Battn was assembled in these trenches about 2pm.	
USNA - TARA Line	2nd	3pm	The Battn received orders to take part in the assault on LA BOISSELLE. AT 3 Coys were ordered to do duty as carrying parties and about 5pm commenced to form a line from our old front line trench across NO MANS-LAND to the village of LA BOISSELLE where the 6 Bn Cheshire Regt. 9th Bn Royal Welsh Fusiliers & 6th Bn Wiltshire Regt had gained a footing, and to pass bombs, ammunition, tools etc up to these troops. The battalion Bombers under command of 2nd Lieut E.R. Kelly had previously (about 4pm) commenced to take part in the assault on the village being attacked to the 9 K Bn Royal Welsh Fusiliers for the time D Company was detailed to dig a communication trench connecting our old front line with the enemy front line at LA BOISSELLE. During is the heavy fire it was found impossible to carry out this task but it was successfully done after dark. Meanwhile this company took part in the work of carrying & passing up supplies to LA BOISSELLE, and parties from A.B.&D Companies were sent up to assist & relieve the bombing parties of the other Battns who were gradually bombing their way up the trenches leading into the village.	
		6pm	B Company was detailed to carry ammunition chiefly for Stokes mortars from the TARA - USNA line to the vicinity of the village.	
		8pm	About 8pm Battalion Headquarters was moved from its position in the TARA - USNA line to TARA redoubt but returned to its original position	
TARA - USNA Line	3	2am	about 2am on July 3rd at 10 am the greater part of C & D boys had been brought back to the TARA - USNA line	

1875 Wt. W593/826 1,000,000 4/15 J.B.C. & A.   A.D.S.S./Forms/C. 2118.

WAR DIARY or INTELLIGENCE SUMMARY

Army Form C. 2118

Place	Date	Hour	Summary of Events and Information	Remarks and references to Appendices
			and the Battalion received orders to move as soon as possible & assist its Brigade in the capture of the village. Battn. H.Q. with C & D Coys, Lewis gun detachments and a proportion of Bombers moved off about 11 am & proceeded via NOTHUMBERLAND AVENUE to the vicinity of our old front line. Firm here, Captain S.W.S. Gardiner &	
		2pm	50 men proceeded to the newly formed craters about X20 A.8.3 the route of advance when given to this party to occupy & commence to consolidate a portion of the old German line from about X20 A.0.5 to X20 B.4.3. This was done	
		3.30pm	about 3.30pm. The Battn. Headquarters & the remainder of C & D Companies & the Lewis gun detachments	
		7pm	moved into this line about 7pm & continued the work of consolidation. D Coy being on the right & C Coy on the left. The line was heavily shelled with shrapnel during the night.	
X20 A.0.5 & X20 B.4.3	4th		The line was extended to the right D Coy taking over another 200 yards of trench to its immediate right. Touch was established with a Battalion of the Yorkshires Regt. (34 Division) on the right and with the 6th Wiltshire Regt. (58th Bde 19th Division) on the left & the work of consolidation continued. The line was subjected to a heavy shelling during the afternoon.	
		9pm	About 9pm the Battalion was ordered to withdraw to the USNA-TARA line and the 56th Brigade had by this time occupied a trench about 300-400 yards east of that held by the Battalion & had joined up on either flank	
		10pm	The two companies accordingly moved out of this line about 10pm & occupied their former positions in the TARA-USNA line during the night. The officer casualties included WOUNDED Capt J.F.G. Gree, Lieut OR J Green (died of wounds) 2nd Lieuts E.R. Kelley & D.L. Davies. The casualties of Other Ranks included 5 killed 77 wounded 5 missing.	866

WAR DIARY or INTELLIGENCE SUMMARY

Army Form C. 2118

Instructions regarding War Diaries and Intelligence Summaries are contained in F. S. Regs., Part II. and the Staff Manual respectively. Title Pages will be prepared in manuscript.

(Erase heading not required.)

Place	Date	Hour	Summary of Events and Information	Remarks and references to Appendices
TARA-USNA Line	5th 6th		The Battalion stood fast in the TARA-USNA trenches. On the morning of the 6th the Battn. received orders to stand by ready to take over a portion of the line near HELIGOLAND with a view to attacking the German line from X15A80 to X16A13. The Battn. moved off at 4.45pm and relieved a Battalion of the WEST YORKSHIRE REGT. the relief being completed at 8.30pm. D Coy occupied the line from X15C01 to X21a79 and B Coy from that point to X15d41. The 23rd Division continued the line to the right but on the left the Germans occupied the line from X14d92 to X14d72. This portion of the line was cleared by a bombing party lead by 2nd Lieut Golding by 11pm and the Battn. thus came into touch with the 56th Brigade which was operating on the left. C + A Coys were kept in support & occupied the line from X21a16 to X21C58. The 5th Battn. Headquarters was at X21C28. A party of bombers from the 5th Battn. sent Walts Borderers under its command of Lieut Hale were attached to the Battn. for the following days operation.	867C
HELIGOLAND 7th		7.30.am	Battn Headquarters was moved into the front line & from X15d O.O. and at the same time A Coy & C Coy moved his the front line + the 6th WILTSHIRE BATTN moved into the support line vacated by these companies. The order of Companies from the right was A.B.C.D.	
		8.15am	the leading platoons of each Company crept over the parapet and were followed by the remaining platoons in succession at the same time, bombing parties detailed by Lieut Hall of the 5th South Wales Borderers proceeded up the communication trenches leading to points X15d25 from 16 points X21a79. X21a92.10 and X15dt2.1. When point 25 was reached they parties were ordered to reform and clean up the trenches up to X15a80 and the various trenches of the starting point around X15 t 81 at the same time bombing parties under 2/Lt 15.S.W.B THOMAS forwarded up the trench leading from X21a4.9 which went to clear that trench up to X15a P.O.	

WAR DIARY or INTELLIGENCE SUMMARY

Army Form C. 2118

Instructions regarding War Diaries and Intelligence Summaries are contained in F.S. Regs., Part II. and the Staff Manual respectively. Title Pages will be prepared in manuscript.

(Erase heading not required.)

Place	Date	Hour	Summary of Events and Information	Remarks and references to Appendices
			The 6th Wiltshire Batn. moved into the first line trenches as soon as they were clear & the 9th Royal Welch Fusiliers moved into the support line. The objective of the Battalion was the trench between X15a80 and X16a1.3. In the advance trench was maintained with the 56th Brigade which was advancing on the left. At about 9.45am the 6th Wiltshire Regt. advanced in support. The two Battalions captured the German line & then proceeded to take up a position from X15 a 5.2 to X15 d 1.3 and proceeded to dig themselves in. An urgent message was sent to the O.C. the 9th Royal Welch Fusiliers asking him to bring his Battn. to the front line with the object of moving forward & filling the gap on the right. He replied that his Battn. were all engaged in the carrying of bombs etc. & that he had applied to the Brigade for the 9th Batn. Cheshire Regt. to be moved forward to relieve him. The attack of the 23rd Durham on the right had failed thus leaving our right flank in the air. Arrangements were made however for two companies of the DURHAM LIGHT INFANTRY to be moved up to extend its line to the right. This was done about 1.30 pm and about 3.30 pm the 9th Bn. ROYAL WELCH FUSILIERS moved up and continued the line to the right to point X15.37.2. During the afternoon a number of casualties were caused by snipers from the rear and it was found that some Germans were still in the stretch between X15 d 2.5 and X15 t 8.1. A bombing party of the Wiltshire Regt. & the Royal Welch Fusiliers cleared the stretch and the Royal Welch Fusiliers extended their line to the right and occupied the string post at X15.48.1. The officer casualties during this action included KILLED 2/Lieut. J.G.B. Stephens. MISSING believed KILLED 2/Lieut. R.B. Bourke. WOUNDED Capt. E.B. Saunders, Lieut. Timm, 2nd Lieuts. Thomas, J.G. Rees, G.H. Golding and Pratt. Other ranks, 178 wounded, 213 killed, 25 missing. In the course of the evening one company of the 9th Cheshire Regt. was moved into the trench between X15 a 9t 0 and X15 d.25 to form a defensive flank.	

1875 Wt. W593/826 1,000,000 4/15 J.B.C. & A. A.D.S.S./Forms/C. 2118.

WAR DIARY
or
INTELLIGENCE SUMMARY
(Erase heading not required.)

Army Form C. 2118.

Place	Date	Hour	Summary of Events and Information	Remarks and references to Appendices
X15d 0.0	8.7.16		The night was quiet & nothing of importance occurred. Nothing of importance happened until about 4.30pm when a number of Germans were observed to be proceeding down the communication trench from X16b49 L5 X16 b25 and thence into CONTALMAISON. There appeared to be a continuous stream of troops and a patrol reported CONTALMAISON to be full of enemy troops. Artillery fire was brought on to the trench in question & subsequently CONTALMAISON was heavily bombarded. It was reported that the enemy suffered heavy casualties. The enemy retaliated by putting up a barrage of artillery fire and bombarding Battalion Headquarters and the line held by the Battalion on the night of the 6/7. Considerable artillery activity continued until 10.30 pm.	
X15d 0.0	9.7.16		The ground held by the various Battalions of the 57th Brigade was taken over by the 112th Brigade in the early hours of this day. This Battn was relieved by a Battn of the WARWICKSHIRE REGT and the relief was completed at 4.0 am. The Battn returned to reserve billets at ALBERT arriving there about 6.30 am at 8.0 pm on the same day the Battalion moved into bivouacs in BAIZEUX WOOD arriving there at 10.30 pm.	
BAIZEUX WOOD	10.7.16		In rest bivouacs	Proceeded to rpt.
do	11.7.16		do	During this period the Brigade was inspected by
do	12.7.16		do	the General Officer commanding III Corps who
do	13.7.16		do	thanked the Brigade for its action
do	14.7.16		do	at LA BOISSELLE
do	15.7.16		do	and "HELIGOLAND"
do	16.7.16		do	
do	17.7.16		do	
do	18.7.16		do	
do	19.7.16		do	

WAR DIARY or INTELLIGENCE SUMMARY

(Erase heading not required.)

Army Form C. 2118

Instructions regarding War Diaries and Intelligence Summaries are contained in F. S. Regs., Part II. and the Staff Manual respectively. Title Pages will be prepared in manuscript.

Place	Date	Hour	Summary of Events and Information	Remarks and references to Appendices
BECOURT WOOD	20th	2.30pm	The Battalion moved via HENIN COURT – MILLEN COURT and ALBERT to BECOURT WOOD where it remained for the night in dugouts & bivouacs	
		5.30am		
	21st	2.30pm	The Battalion proceeded by half companies via FRICOURT & SUNKEN road and went into bivouacs & old german trenches in the Southern end of MAMETZ WOOD	
MAMETZ WOOD		5.30am		
	22nd		The Battalion stood fast in MAMETZ wood. Officers proceeded to Eastern edge of wood to reconnoitre ground in front. About 3.30 pm The Southern edge of the wood was subjected to a most intense bombardment with shrapnel and H.E. probably from 5.9" Howitzers, followed at about half hour intervals by three others of similar intensity. The Battalion was well dug in & in consequence only suffered about twenty casualties.	
"		8pm	In consequence the Battalion moved to a position about X24A/3 near the centre of the road where it occupied dugouts & bivouacs during the night.	
BAZENTIN LE PETIT.	23	8/am	The Battn moved off by ½ Companies at 8am & relieved the 8th NORTH STAFFORD- SHIRE Regt (57th Brigade). Position mainly as follows A & B + C Coys occupied a line of trenches roughly from about S.90.7.9. leaving just N of the midline at S.94.0 and thence running along the track to "Five Ways" about S.83.5.8. D Coy held a support trench from the cemetery at S.8.D7½.9 to S.8.54.2. Battn headquarters were situated in the quarry just NE. of the cemetery (about S.88.9)	
		10.30pm	The relief was completed about 10.30 pm without incident. The Battn was	

1875 Wt. W593/826 1,000,000 4/15 J.B.C. & A. A.D.S.S./Forms/C. 2118.

WAR DIARY or INTELLIGENCE SUMMARY

Army Form C. 2118

Place	Date	Hour	Summary of Events and Information	Remarks and references to Appendices
BAZENTIN LE PETIT.			now in support to the 9th Royal Welch Fusiliers occupying a front line but facing mainly north west. The 6" Wiltshire Regt. was in touch with the left of 119 Battalion and held a line mainly running E & W just north of the village of BAZENTIN LE PETIT. The 51st Division was on the right but immediate touch with any Battalion was not established although a line of trenches was gradually being established between the right of the Battalion and HIGH WOOD. Touch was on this flank however established with posts & Lewis Gun detachments of a Battalion of Argyll & Sutherland Highlanders which had established itself about S.9 central.	
	24.7.16		The day was without incident except for two very heavy German barrages directed on our lines about 4 p.m. & 8.30 p.m. The latter lasted nearly 3 hours and was most intense. During this period about 30 casualties were suffered by the Battalion.	
	25 26 27		During this period the following alterations took place in the position of the Battalion. A new line of trenches commenced by the 5th Bn South Wales Borderers & completed by 'C' Coy was dug from S3C1:2 thus forming a continuation of the Fusiliers on the left about S3C1:2 thus forming a continuation of the front line on the night of the 9th Bn Royal Welch Fusiliers. This new trench was occupied by C Company. From which touch was established on the right of our original line with the 51st Division. About the end of this period the 51st Division commenced to complete & occupy a shallow trench running from the right of our new front line described above towards HIGH WOOD	

War Diary 9th Welsh Regt July 1916

Summary of Events and Information

Place	Date	Hour	
	28th		A great deal of work was done during these days in making or improving new communication trenches & in the existing trenches & in the vicinity. The Battalion was ordered to seize & occupy the German strong post at S30 B.5 at 9.45pm & to hold it during the following day, with Lewis guns & a small party. Parties from 'B' Coy with bombers & Lewis gunners were assembled in the front trenches ready for this enterprise, but at 9.30pm our artillery activity commenced. In both sides & the German barrage which was most intense although ineffective prevented any patrol work in front of the line, and any movement whatever outside our trenches. In consequence the enterprise had to be abandoned & parties remained their companies.
BAZENTIN LE PETIT	29th	3.30pm	Following a bombardment by our 9.2" howitzers on the strong post at S30 B.5 the enemy barraged our lines for about half an hour but ineffectually
		5pm	At 5pm the Battalion started to move from the trenches being relieved by the 7th KING'S OWN Regt on the right of our line & by the 10th ROYAL WARWICKSHIRES Regt on the left. The relief was completed about 7pm & the Battalion
BECOURT WOOD		7pm	marched in small parties to BECOURT WOOD where it bivouacked for the night
BETHEN COURT	30th	12nn	The Battalion moved at noon & proceeded by Companies to rest billets at BETHEN COURT via ALBERT, ALBERT – AMIENS road and FRANVILLERS.

J.L. Cooke Luxted
Comdg. 9th Welsh Regt

VOL 12

58th Brigade.
19th Division.

1/9th BATTALION

THE WELCH REGIMENT

AUGUST 1 9 1 6

Army Form C. 2118.

WAR DIARY
or
INTELLIGENCE SUMMARY.

(Erase heading not required.)

58/5 Vol 12

9th Service Battalion The Welch Regiment

War Diary

August 1916.

WAR DIARY
or
INTELLIGENCE SUMMARY.
(Erase heading not required.)

Army Form C. 2118.

Place	Date	Hour	Summary of Events and Information	Remarks and references to Appendices
BEHENCOURT	1.8.16		In Billets at BEHENCOURT	
do	2.8.16			
do	3.8.16		The Battalion entrained at FRECHENCOURT and proceeded via AMIENS to LONGPRÉ whence they marched to Billets at PONT REMY	
PONT REMY	4.8.16		In Billets at PONT REMY	
do	5.8.16			
do	6.8.16		The Battalion entrained at Pont Remy at 6.0 pm and proceeded by train to BAILLEUL	
BAILLEUL	7.8.16	3.0 am	The Battalion detrained and marched to camp at M.18.d.8.2. where it rested until 8.30 pm	
		8.30 pm	The Battalion moved into Brigade Reserve at R.C. FARM at N.15.c.2.6.	
R.C. FARM	8.8.16		In Brigade Reserve	
	9.8.16			
	10.8.16			
	11.8.16			
	12.8.16			

Army Form C. 2118.

WAR DIARY
or
INTELLIGENCE SUMMARY.
(Erase heading not required.)

Instructions regarding War Diaries and Intelligence Summaries are contained in F. S. Regs., Part II. and the Staff Manual respectively. Title pages will be prepared in manuscript.

Place	Date	Hour	Summary of Events and Information	Remarks and references to Appendices
RC. FARM.	13.8.16	11.30 pm	The Battalion relieved the 6th Batt. Wiltshire Regt. in the line from N24d 3½ 7½ to N18c 4 2. B Coy were in the front line on the right and D Coy on the Left. A Coy in support in K1A and TURNERSTOWN and C Coy in Reserve in ROSSIGNOL WOOD, FORT HALIFAX and FORT ROYAL	
	14.8.16		In the line as above.	
	15.8.16			
	16.8.16		The enemy attempted a raid on the Battalion front on the night of the 17/18. The party consisted of about 12 one man was captured & two were killed. It is Rough Kent no further trouble occurred.	
	17.8.16			
	18.8.16			
	19.8.16	midnight 12.0	The Battalion was relieved in the line by the 6th Batt. Wiltshire Regt. and proceeded to the Butterfly Camp at N19A in Divisional Reserve	
BUTTERFLY CAMP	20.8.16		In Divisional Reserve as above	
	21.8.16			
	22.8.16			
	23.8.16			
	24.8.16			

Army Form C. 2118.

WAR DIARY
or
INTELLIGENCE SUMMARY.
(Erase heading not required.)

Instructions regarding War Diaries and Intelligence Summaries are contained in F.S. Regs., Part II. and the Staff Manual respectively. Title pages will be prepared in manuscript.

Place	Date	Hour	Summary of Events and Information	Remarks and references to Appendices
BUTTERFLY CAMP.	25.8.16	midnight 12:0	The Battalion relieved the 6th Bn Wiltshire Regt in the line. A Coy in the front line on the right. C Coy in the front line on the left. B Coy in Support & D in Reserve	
ROSSIGNOL	26.8.16		} In line as above.	
	27.8.16			
	28.8.16			
	29.8.16			
	30.8.16			
	31.8.16		The Battn was relieved by the 6th Bn Wiltshire Regt and retired to Brigade Reserve at R.C. FARM.	

J. L. Cooke
Lieut-Colonel
Comdg 9th Bn The Welch Regt.

1st Sept. 1916.

Army Form C. 2118.

VOL 13

WAR DIARY
or
INTELLIGENCE SUMMARY.
(Erase heading not required.)

9th Ser. Batn The Welch Regiment.

War Diary.

September 1916.

Army Form C. 2118.

WAR DIARY
or
INTELLIGENCE SUMMARY.
(Erase heading not required.)

Instructions regarding War Diaries and Intelligence Summaries are contained in F. S. Regs., Part II. and the Staff Manual respectively. Title pages will be prepared in manuscript.

Place	Date	Hour	Summary of Events and Information	Remarks and references to Appendices
R.C. FARM.	1.9.16		In Brigade Reserve.	
do	2.9.16			
do	3.9.16		The Battalion was relieved by a Battalion of the 12th Canadian Brigade and marched into billets at LOCRE.	
LOCRE.	4.9.16	2.0 p	The Battalion moved by road via DRANOUTRE & B1 central to NIEPPE and neighbourhood. Battn. Headquarters at PONT NIEPPE	
NIEPPE	5.9.16		In reserve in NIEPPE area	
do	6.9.16			
do	7.9.16			
do	8.9.16		The Battn. relieved the 9th Royal Scots in the line from C.16 d 2.6 to ESSEX FARM (C.16.a.7.1) B. C. & D Coys were in the front line, B on the right, C in the centre & D on the left. A Coy was in support. Bn. Headquarters was at Surrey Headquarters FARM	
SURREY HQ FARM.	9.9.16			
	10.9.16		In the line as above	
	11.9.16			
	12.9.16			

WAR DIARY
or
INTELLIGENCE SUMMARY.

(Erase heading not required.)

Army Form C. 2118.

Place	Date	Hour	Summary of Events and Information	Remarks and references to Appendices
SURREY HQ FARM	13.9.16		The Battalion was relieved by the 6th Wiltshire Battalion & proceeded into Brigade Reserve at CHAPPELLE ROMPUE C7&Q3. D Coy manned the posts at PATERNOSTER ROW, RESERVE FARM, FORT PAUL & GUNNER FARM. A Coy held LYS FARM, STATION REDOUBT + SEVEN TREES REDOUBT.	
CHAPPELLE ROMPUE	14.9.16		In reserve as above. Working parties consisting of about 100 men were furnished by B & C Coys daily for work under the R.E's.	
do	15.9.16			
do	16.9.16			
do	17.9.16			
do	18.9.16			
do	19.9.16			
do	20.9.16		The Battn was relieved by the 8' Devons and moved via BAILLEUL to billets in the OUTERSTEENE – STRAZEELE AREA for training. Battn Headquarters at Sheet 36a F.2.&.5.9.	
OUTERSTEENE	21.9.16		In Training as above	
	22.9.16			
	23.9.16			

Army Form C. 2118.

WAR DIARY
or
INTELLIGENCE SUMMARY.
(Erase heading not required.)

Instructions regarding War Diaries and Intelligence Summaries are contained in F. S. Regs., Part II. and the Staff Manual respectively. Title pages will be prepared in manuscript.

Place	Date	Hour	Summary of Events and Information	Remarks and references to Appendices
OUTERSTEENE	24.9.16			
	25.9.16		In Training as above.	
	26.9.16			
	27.9.16			
	28.9.16			
	29.9.16			
	30.9.16			

2.10.16.

L. Stephens Major
Commands 6th Bn Black Watch Regt

T.2134. Wt. W708—776. 500000. 4/15. Sir J. C. & S.

Army Form C. 2118.

Vol 14

WAR DIARY
or
INTELLIGENCE SUMMARY.
(Erase heading not required.)

9th (Sr) Batt. The Welch Regiment

War Diary

October 1916

WAR DIARY
or
INTELLIGENCE SUMMARY.

(Erase heading not required.)

Army Form C. 2118.

Place	Date	Hour	Summary of Events and Information	Remarks and references to Appendices
OUTERSTEENE	1-10-16		On training and refitting in billets in the OUTERSTEENE – STRAZEELE Area	
do	2-10-16			
do	3-10-16			
do	4-10-16			
do	5-10-16	16:15	The Battalion moved from their billets to BAILLEUL WEST STATION and proceeded to entrain	
		18:45	Entrainment completed	
		19.28	Left BAILLEUL WEST STATION en route for DOULLENS.	
DOULLENS	6-10-16	3:30	Arrived DOULLENS detrainment finished by 4:30 and Battalion marched to bivouacs in BOIS de WARNIMONT I.24 central. Blankets were issued en route. Arrived here at 9.0	
			The entraining strength of the Battalion was 30 officers and 829 other Ranks	
WARNIMONT	7-10-16	9.0	The Battalion marched off via ST LEGER – COIGNEUX – SAILLY – X Roads HEBUTERNE to relieve the 1/6 Seaforth Highlanders in the line from K.17a 5.7 to K.17c. A & B Coys occupied the front line C Coy in Support and D Coy in Reserve	

WAR DIARY
or
INTELLIGENCE SUMMARY.

(Erase heading not required.)

Army Form C. 2118.

Instructions regarding War Diaries and Intelligence Summaries are contained in F. S. Regs., Part II. and the Staff Manual respectively. Title pages will be prepared in manuscript.

Place	Date	Hour	Summary of Events and Information	Remarks and references to Appendices
HEBUTERNE	8-10-16		On the line as above - a great deal of reconnaissance work was done and preparations made with a view to offensive operation	
do	9-10-16		The Battalion was relieved by the 9th Bn Cheshire Regt. and proceeded into Bivouacs near SAILLY-AU-BOIS.	
	10-10-16		In bivouacs as above. A large number of working parties were supplied for work under the R.E.'s and all available time was spent in training operations, especially practising to follow an artillery Barrage	
	11-10-16			
	12-10-16			
	13-10-16			
	14-10-16			
	15-10-16			
	16-10-16		The Battalion was relieved by the 10th Bn East Yorks Regt (92nd Brigade) and proceeded by bus to huts at VAUCHELLES.	
VAUCHELLES	17-10-16		The Battalion was ordered to move off by road to HERISART via RAINCHEVAL and TOUTENCOURT at 10.38 am but was blocked by the 19th Divisional artillery and the D.A.C. and could not start until 12.30. The Battalion arrived in billets at HERISART at 16.0	

WAR DIARY
or
INTELLIGENCE SUMMARY.
(Erase heading not required.)

Army Form C. 2118.

Instructions regarding War Diaries and Intelligence Summaries are contained in F. S. Regs., Part II. and the Staff Manual respectively. Title pages will be prepared in manuscript.

Place	Date	Hour	Summary of Events and Information	Remarks and references to Appendices
HERISART	18-10-16		In Billets as above	
	19-10-16			
	20-10-16			
	21-10-16	9.7	The Battalion moved to BOUZINCOURT arriving in billets here at 13:15.	
BOUZINCOURT	22-10-16	9.0	The Battalion moved from its Billets to Reserve Camps at W.8 central and furnished 400 men to carry artillery ammunition	
RESERVE CAMP	23-10-16		In Reserve as above	
	24-10-16			
	25-10-16			
do	26-10-16	10:30	The Battalion moved off to relieve the 8th Loyal North Lancashire Regt in the front line from about R.20 a 1.1 to 6.1. B Coy held the front line in STUFF TRENCH. A Coy in support along the LUCKY WAY and SPLUTTER RD. C & D Coys in reserve in BAINBRIDGE and RANSOME TRENCHES respectively. Bn HQ in BULGAR TRENCH at R20 c 7.1	
		15:30	Relief completed.	
		23:30	Information received that the enemy was preparing to attack from the	

WAR DIARY
or
INTELLIGENCE SUMMARY.
(Erase heading not required.)

Army Form C. 2118.

Place	Date	Hour	Summary of Events and Information	Remarks and references to Appendices
			direction of the LUCKY WAY with the 9th Regiment in the morning of the 27th. Lewis Guns were placed in front of the line in readiness for such an eventuality. There was considerable artillery activity during the day.	
	27-10-16		In the line as above. The enemy did not counter-attack. Considerable artillery activity during the day.	
		12·0	Casualties for the previous 24 hours. Officers NIL. Other Ranks KILLED 3. WOUNDED 11.	
	28-10-16		In the line as above. Artillery activity heavy and continuous.	
		12·0	Casualties for the previous 24 hours. Officers NIL. Other Ranks WOUNDED 5.	
	29-10-16		In the line as above. Casualties up to 12 noon. Officers NIL. Other Ranks KILLED one. WOUNDED one. 2nd Lieutenants B.S.M. Ronas and G. Fitzsimmons and a party of 20 men some of whom were Lewis Gunners, Scouts & Snipers, successfully bombed a strong point at R.20.a 5½ 2¼	

Army Form C. 2118.

WAR DIARY
or
INTELLIGENCE SUMMARY.
(Erase heading not required.)

Instructions regarding War Diaries and Intelligence Summaries are contained in F. S. Regs., Part II. and the Staff Manual respectively. Title pages will be prepared in manuscript.

Place	Date	Hour	Summary of Events and Information	Remarks and references to Appendices
	30-10-16		The Battalion was relieved in the line by the 7th Bn. North Lancashire Regt and proceeded into Bivouacs at DONNETTS POST. W.12.D. Relief completed at 13.0	
	31-10-16		In Bivouacs as above	

J. D. Crookenden Lieut Colonel
Comdg 9th (S) Bn. The Welch Regt

Army Form C. 2118.

WAR DIARY
or
INTELLIGENCE SUMMARY.

(Erase heading not required.)

58/9   Vol 15

9th (Sev) Bn The Welch Regiment

War Diary

November 1916.

WAR DIARY
or
INTELLIGENCE SUMMARY.
(Erase heading not required.)

Army Form C. 2118.

Place	Date	Hour	Summary of Events and Information	Remarks and references to Appendices
Donnetts Post Bulgar Trench	1.11.16		The Battalion remained in Camp at Donnetts Post. W.12.D	
	2.11.16		The Battalion moved into the line. Battn Headquarters in Bulgar Trench. D Coy in front line, C in support in SPLUTTER ROAD, A Coy in RANSOME TRENCH & B Coy in BAINBRIDGE TRENCH.	
do	3.11.16		In the line as above.	
do	4.11.16		In the line as above. A Coy relieved D Coy in the front line & D Coy moved back in RANSOME TRENCH	
do	5.11.16		The Battn was relieved by the 7th North Lancashire Regt & proceeded to dug-outs. A, B & C Coys in LEIPZIG REDOUBT. & D Coy in WOOD POST. The Battalion was in close support of the left of the Divisional front.	
Wood Post	6.11.16			
do	7.11.16		In close Support. as above.	
do	8.11.16			
do	9.11.16			
do	10.11.16			

WAR DIARY
or
INTELLIGENCE SUMMARY.
(Erase heading not required.)

Army Form C. 2118.

Place	Date	Hour	Summary of Events and Information	Remarks and references to Appendices
Wood Post.	17.11.16		The Battalion moved into dugouts in X.2.a. x X.2.c (Old German) front line where it was in close support of the Right Sector of the Brigade front.	
X.2.a.	18.11.16		In close support as above.	
Stuff Redoubt	18/19.11.16		The Battalion relieved the 6th Wiltshire Regt. in the line at STUFF REDOUBT. A, B, & 3 platoons of B Coy in the front line extending from about 200 yards to the right of STUMP ROAD to the junction of OG1 & STUFF TRENCH at R30 c.8.9.5. 3 platoons of A Coy occupying the line to the right of STUMP ROAD. One platoon of C Coy was in support in O.G.2. x B Coy in RESERVE in ZOLLERN TRENCH	
"	19.11.16		A Coy under Lieut. J. Gibbons assisted by Lieut. A.D. Williams & 2/Lt. Young formed a raiding party to clean the dugouts along STUMP ROAD up to & including the point where DESIRE TRENCH crossed the STUMP ROAD. The company was divided into three parties. The first under Lieut. A.D. Williams which followed the barrage closely, the second under 2/Lt. W.R.B. Young & the third under Lieut. J. Gibbons completed the cleaning up process	

WAR DIARY or INTELLIGENCE SUMMARY

Army Form C. 2118.

Place	Date	Hour	Summary of Events and Information	Remarks and references to Appendices
			The parties dealt with three dugouts and partially dealt with a fourth and inflicted heavy casualties on the enemy. The leading platoon however came up against a German strong point near the junction of DESIRE TRENCH & STUMP ROAD & a German machine gun got into action near this point. Several casualties were caused & the parties withdrew. Casualties Wounded Lieuts J.K.Jones & D.Williams, 20 other ranks wounded 10 O.R. wounded & missing. 2 O.R. missing.	
Stuff Redoubt	15.11.16		In the line as above	
do	16.11.16		In the line as above. Three platoons of "A" coy occupying the portion of the line to the right of STUMP ROAD were relieved by a Battalion of the 18th Division & proceeded to dugouts in old German front line at X.2.a X.2.c. 2/Lt J.K.Jones was killed by a sniper. 2/Lt Whitelam wounded.	
do	17.11.16		The Battalion was relieved by the 8th North Staffordshire Regt & proceeded into dugouts in old German front line in X.2.a X.2.c.	
X.2.a Wellington Huts	18.11.16		The Battalion moved into WELLINGTON HUTS W.12.D	
	19.11.16	11.30	The Battalion received orders to proceed into SUPPORT, in	

WAR DIARY
or
INTELLIGENCE SUMMARY.
(Erase heading not required.)

Army Form C. 2118.

Place	Date	Hour	Summary of Events and Information	Remarks and references to Appendices
			BULGAR and BAINBRIDGE TRENCHES & moved off at 2.30 p.m.	
		4.30	Orders received to take over the front line STUFF TRENCH from STUMP ROAD to the junction of STUFF TRENCH & O.G.1. R.20.6-85. Relief completed 10.36 p.m.	
Stuff Redoubt	20.11.16			
do	21.11.16		In the line as above	
do	22.11.16		The Battalion was relieved by a Company of the 8th Northumberland Fusiliers and proceeded to WELLINGTON HUTS. Relief completed 8.30 p.m.	
Wellington Huts	23.11.16		The Battalion moves partly by motor lorries & partly by road to WARLOY where it occupied billets. 336 O.R. were taken by lorries	
Warloy	24.11.16		The Battalion marched from WARLOY to Billets at Doullens, 1500 R were conveyed by train from ACHEUX to GEZAINCOURT.	
Doullens	25.11.16		The Battn marched to HEUZECOURT arriving there 12.30 p.m.	
HEUZECOURT	26.11.16			
do	27.11.16		In Billets at HEUZECOURT.	
do	28.11.16			

Army Form C. 2118.

WAR DIARY
or
INTELLIGENCE SUMMARY.
(Erase heading not required.)

Instructions regarding War Diaries and Intelligence Summaries are contained in F. S. Regs., Part II. and the Staff Manual respectively. Title pages will be prepared in manuscript.

Place	Date	Hour	Summary of Events and Information	Remarks and references to Appendices
HEUZECOURT	29th		In Billets at HEUZECOURT.	
do	30 n.m			

Lablette. Major
Comdg 19th Bn The Welsh Regt.

Army Form C. 2118.

WAR DIARY
or
INTELLIGENCE SUMMARY.

(Erase heading not required.)

Vol 16

9th (Sev) Battalion. The Welch Regiment.

War Diary.

December 1916.

WAR DIARY
or
INTELLIGENCE SUMMARY.
(Erase heading not required.)

Army Form C. 2118.

Place	Date	Hour	Summary of Events and Information	Remarks and references to Appendices
ECOURT	Dec 1st to 30 31st		The battalion was billeted at HEUDECOURT and was enjoyed slowslow the month in Section, Platoon & Company drawing	

Godfrey Lieut Col
O/C 9th Welch Regt

Army Form C. 2118.

WAR DIARY
or
INTELLIGENCE SUMMARY.
(Erase heading not required.)

Vol 17

1st Ben Battalion The Welsh Regiment.

War Diary

January 1917.

Army Form C. 2118.

WAR DIARY
or
INTELLIGENCE-SUMMARY.
(Erase heading not required.)

Place	Date	Hour	Summary of Events and Information	Remarks and references to Appendices
HEBUTERNE	Jan. 1-8th		The Battalion was engaged in training at HEBUTERNE	
	9th		On Jan. 9th the Battalion moved to billets in BEAUVAL, and remained there in 10th.	
	11th		The Battalion moved by motor lorry to ROSSIGNOL FARM - COIGNEUX where it was in Brigade Reserve	
	19th		The Battalion relieved the 6th Wiltshire Regt. in L2 Sub Sector of the HEBUTERNE Sector of the line - Coy 3 Coys in front line 1R & B in Support.	
	23rd		The Battalion was relieved by the 6th Welsh Regt. & moved to the DELL	
	27th		Battalion relieves 6th Welsh in L2 Sector, At B Coys in front line et D in Support	
	28th		On night of 29/30th the a patrol reconnoitred the POINT with a view to a raid. The German wire was found to be much damaged by artillery fire. About 7 Germans were encountered & casualties were inflicted upon them. The patrol returned without loss.	

WAR DIARY
or
INTELLIGENCE SUMMARY.
(Erase heading not required.)

Army Form C. 2118.

Place	Date	Hour	Summary of Events and Information	Remarks and references to Appendices
THE LINE	29th & 30th		On the nights of 29/30 & 30/31 a raiding party entered the German line near the Point. The party consisted of 2 officers & 30 OR with a covering party - two Lewis guns were also taken. The Germans were either lying in wait for the raid or were about to raid our lines. When between two German holes our party encountered a very large party of Germans - these were successfully dealt with by the Lewis guns which were fired at a range of 15 yards. The German fire were bombers & our party which was greatly inferior in numbers, to the enemy retired without loss to our lines, covered by Lewis gun fire. Another raid on night of 29/30th was made in a German trenches - probably a deserter.	
	31st		Battalion was relieved in the line by 6: Will. Brigny Lieut Col Commanding Welch Regt	

Army Form C. 2118.

Vol 18

WAR DIARY
or
INTELLIGENCE SUMMARY.
(Erase heading not required.)

WAR DIARY

9th (Service) Battalion The Welch Regiment.

February 1917.

Army Form C. 2118.

WAR DIARY
or
INTELLIGENCE SUMMARY.
(Erase heading not required.)

Instructions regarding War Diaries and Intelligence Summaries are contained in F.S. Regs., Part II. and the Staff Manual respectively. Title pages will be prepared in manuscript.

Place	Date	Hour	Summary of Events and Information	Remarks and references to Appendices
BAILLY AU BOIS	1st		The Battalion were billeted in Brigade Reserve in the DELL BAILLY AU BOIS	
THE DELL	4th		The Battalion relieved the 6th Wilts' Regiment in the line. Companies were disposed as follows of the HEBUTERNE Section of the line. Companies were Suffolk" C by Right front D by Left front.	
COURCELLES	9th		The Battalion was relieved by the 9th Cheshire Regt and moved to billets at COURCELLES	
COIGNEUX	10		The Battalion moved into huts vacated by 5th S.W.Borderers at J.16.A.57 near COIGNEUX. The Battalion were engaged in practising the various attack formations	
BUS EN ARTOIS	19		The Battalion moved from huts at J.16.A.57 into billets at BUS EN ARTOIS	
COURCELLES	27		The Battalion moved from BUS to COURCELLES	

WAR DIARY
or
INTELLIGENCE SUMMARY.

(Erase heading not required.)

Army Form C. 2118.

Place	Date	Hour	Summary of Events and Information	Remarks and references to Appendices
THE LINE	28.		info overlay to going with the line. The Bn relieved the 10th Warwicks and two companies of 10th Worcesters in the line evacuated by the Germans between PUISIEUX and ROSSIGNOL WOOD.	

W Humphrey Lt Col.
Comdg. 9' Bn W ch Regt

Army Form C. 2118.

No 19

WAR DIARY
or
INTELLIGENCE SUMMARY.
(Erase heading not required.)

9th Service Battalion the Welch Regiment.

War Diary.

March 1917.

WAR DIARY
or
INTELLIGENCE SUMMARY.

(Erase heading not required.)

Army Form C. 2118.

Place	Date	Hour	Summary of Events and Information	Remarks and references to Appendices
THE LINE	12th		The dispositions of the Battalion in the line were as follows (reference attached map squares L13 and 14) A Coy were in Sufflurl in STAR ALLEY. B, C & D Coys were holding the front line ROSSIGNOL TRENCH as follows:- B Coy on right were holding from L13.D.7.9 to L14.A.12.2. C Coy on left of B Coy from L13.D.7.9 to L13.B.0.5. D Coy on left of line from L13.B.0.5 to L13.A.24.5. The enemy were holding the line as follows: on our left flank they held strong bombing posts at L13.A.38 and L13.A.49 - they held BERG GRABEN and its continuation (now called ST DAVIDS TRENCH and so marked on attached map), KNIFE and FORK TRENCHES. Strong bombing posts had been established by them at L14.A.22.41 and L14.A.31.41. BLUE STREET was held by the enemy bombing attacks from his posts on our flanks had not been successful. B Coy attempts to clear the enemy further up KNIFE and FORK TRENCHES on the morning of 12th, but the Germans familiarly with all the trench system is the rear and flanks counfalled our progress to be very slow. It was therefore decided to attack the enemy own the afore as far as possible during the night of 12th/13th. The objective being (1) to clear the enemy from KNIFE and FORK TRENCHES as far as	by the enemy

WAR DIARY
or
INTELLIGENCE SUMMARY

Army Form C. 2118.

Place	Date	Hour	Summary of Events and Information	Remarks and references to Appendices
	1st		the junction of FORK TRENCH and ST DAVID'S TRENCH and to establish bombing posts, also to capture the line L.13.A.0.7 through finds 3.8 and d.9 to junction of the trench with ST DAVIDS TRENCH (2) if possible to establish a front line in ST DAVIDS TRENCH. The objective was alloted to Companies as follows B Coy were ordered to capture KNIFE and FORK TRENCHES, to establish bombing posts all the finds mentioned and then to push along ST DAVID'S TRENCH from the East-D Coy were to capture finds 3.8 and d.9 also the trench north of find 3.8 and to push along ST DAVIDS TRENCH from the West to gain touch with B Coy and to establish a line of posts along ST DAVIDS TRENCH. A Coy were to capture the line from find 3.8 to L.13.A.0.7 to gain touch with D Coy and also with 31st Division who were to attack SIDE STREET from DUGOUT LANE and were to remain in touch with us at L.13.A.0.7. C Coy were ordered to remain in reserve in ROSSIGNOL TRENCH which would form the new support line after the attack. Zero hour was fixed for 12 midnight. Ten minutes before zero the artillery were to open a lyddite barrage with 18 pdrs on ST DAVIDS TRENCH and the heavy artillery was to fire on FBRK	

WAR DIARY
or
INTELLIGENCE SUMMARY.
(Erase heading not required.)

Army Form C. 2118.

Place	Date	Hour	Summary of Events and Information	Remarks and references to Appendices
			WOOD and BERG GRABEN. Stokes Mortars were to co-operate by firing on the enemy's bombing posts at KNIFE and FORK TRENCHES and on points 38 and 49. B by encountered a good deal of resistance from the Germans in KNIFE TRENCH about L13 B 9.9 - at this point the enemy had safeguards at the bend in the trench. A by reached their objective encountering little resistance but could gain no touch with Battalion on their left - their objective was same about 1.30 am. D by after encountering some resistance at points # 38 and 49 reached the junction of ST DAVIDS TRENCH and at 4.35 am had pushed up the trench for a distance of 150 yards. It was however so dark that it was decided to wait till daybreak to gain touch with B by. B by P/ 4.45 am B by had also reached ST DAVIDS TRENCH and were prepared to gain touch with D by at daybreak. This was done and a line of posts were established early in the morning of 2nd. After this the Germans down to BLUE STREET and had established a full barrage at K18 B 7.6 the Battalion on our left gained touch with us about 10.0 am. Casualties amounted to 1 officer wounded & OR Killed 32 OR wounded. Battalion was relieved by 6" Wells in line and moved to billets in COOREULES	

Army Form C. 2118

WAR DIARY
or
INTELLIGENCE SUMMARY.
(Erase heading not required.)

Instructions regarding War Diaries and Intelligence Summaries are contained in F.S. Regs., Part II. and the Staff Manual respectively. Title pages will be prepared in manuscript.

Place	Date	Hour	Summary of Events and Information	Remarks and references to Appendices
	3.		Battalion moved to billets at BUS.	
	10.		Battalion began its march from V Army to II Army area - moving to BEAUVAL.	
	11.		Battalion moved to NEUVILLETE	
	13.		Battalion moved to FRAMECOURT	
	15.		Battalion moved to MAREST	
	16.		Battalion moved to RELY	
	17.		Battalion moved to billets near AIRE	
	18.		Battalion moved to MERRIS	
	20.		Battalion moved to billets near FLETRE	
	22.		A B & D Coys went Detached for work on railway near DRANOUTRE	
	31.		Battalion moved to MORRON BRIDGE CAMP near LA CLYTTE in reserve to two Battalions in line in DIEPENDAL Sector of line near ST ELOI	

Army Form C. 2118.

WAR DIARY
or
INTELLIGENCE SUMMARY.
(Erase heading not required.)

9th Battalion The Welch Regiment

War Diary

April 1917

Army Form C. 2118.

WAR DIARY
or
INTELLIGENCE SUMMARY.
(Erase heading not required.)

Instructions regarding War Diaries and Intelligence
Summaries are contained in F.S. Regs., Part II.
and the Staff Manual respectively. Title pages
will be prepared in manuscript.

Place	Date	Hour	Summary of Events and Information	Remarks and references to Appendices
Line	April 4		Battalion relieved 9th Bn. Cheshire Regt in Right Subsect of DICKEBUSH Sect of the Line	
	8		The Battalion was relieved in the line by 9' R.W.F. & moved to RIDGE WOOD in close support of the line	
	12		Bn relieved 9' R.W.F. in line	
	16		The Battalion was relieved by 6' Welsh Regt and moved to CURRAGH Camp near LA CLYTTE. Three hundred men were detached for work on Railway at KERSEBROM.	
	19		Bn less 300 men moved to billets near BERTHEN in the BOESCHEPE Training area	
BERTHEN	24		300 men rejoined from work on railway	
	30		Bn received orders to move immediately to ST LAWRENCE Camp between POPERINGHE and VLAMERTINGHE to relieve 69' Bde 23rd Division in the SALIENT.	

R.C.J. Kempthorne Colonel
Comdg. 9th (Sev) Batn. the Welsh Regt.

Army Form C. 2118.

WAR DIARY
or
INTELLIGENCE SUMMARY.
(Erase heading not required.)

Vol 21

9th (Ser) Battalion The Welch Regiment

War Diary

May 1917

WAR DIARY
or
INTELLIGENCE SUMMARY.

(Erase heading not required.)

Army Form C. 2118.

Place	Date	Hour	Summary of Events and Information	Remarks and references to Appendices
Line	1st W		The Battalion relieved 10th Northumberland Fusiliers 23rd Division in their 2nd/half of ZILLEBEKE Sector of the line, Battalion HQ at "TUILERIES". A & B Coys in trenches C & D Coys in YPRES.	
	11th		Battalion relieved 9th R107 in left subsector ZILLEBEKE sector, C & D Coys in line A & B Coys in support.	
	12th		The Battalion was relieved by 9th York Lancs. 23rd Division. moved to HALIFAX Camp.	
	13th		Battalion moved to billets at BERTHEN.	
	15th		Battalion marched to 34 RCOs en route to RECQUES training area.	
	16th		" " WIZERNES	
	17th		Battalion reaches MONTROLE	
	18th to 24th		Battalion training, attack in 2nd Army Training area — 2 Drafts of 60 and 40 were sent up to the Battalion during this time.	

WAR DIARY
or
INTELLIGENCE SUMMARY.

Army Form C. 2118.

Place	Date	Hour	Summary of Events and Information	Remarks and references to Appendices
	25		Battalion moved to CARNARVON Camp in SCHERPENBERG area, entraining at WATTEN and detraining at BRILLEUL.	
	26		Battalion moved to MORRE π BIDGER Camp & Ruffles now being for tea for infantry assembly trenches etc in DIEPENDAHL Sector.	

[signature]

Army Form C. 2118.

WAR DIARY
or
INTELLIGENCE SUMMARY.
(Erase heading not required.)

9th (Ser) Battalion The Welch Regiment

War Diary.

June 1917.

WAR DIARY or INTELLIGENCE SUMMARY

Army Form C. 2118.

Place	Date	Hour	Summary of Events and Information	Remarks and references to Appendices
	June 3rd		The Battalion took over the Right Subsector of the line in relief of 6" Wilts Regt - The continuous bombardment of the German line preparatory to the attack on the WYTSCHAETE - MESSINES ridge having commenced on the previous day.	
	5th		The Battalion was relieved in the line by 2 Companies 9' RWF and 2 coys 6' Wilts Regt: on relief moved to MURRUMBIDGEE Camp IS complete final equipment for the attack. Zero day fixes for June 7".	
	6th		Battalion moved from MURRUMBIDGEE Camp IS the Suffolk, have Assembly trenches which were the Suffolk line and a tunnel - fir day dirmally behind N. Disposition in Assembly were as follows: A by in Suffolk Trench on right of POPPY LANE (OC A Cy Capt PD Buxton) - B by in Suffolk Trench on left of POPPY LANE (OC B Cy Capt EB Saunders) C & D coys intervening to in tunnel fut on right and left of POPPY LANE (OC C Cy Capt G Fitz Simmons - OC D Cy 2/Lt JA Fy Gilbert) Zero hour 3.10 am. Assembly completed 12.15 am. Appendix A (Operation Orders for the Battalion) gives the objectives	

Army Form C. 2118.

WAR DIARY
or
INTELLIGENCE SUMMARY.
(Erase heading not required.)

Place	Date	Hour	Summary of Events and Information	Remarks
	7.	3.30am	and Dispositions of the Battalion in full. The Battalion left the Assembly Trenches at 3.30 am – the enemy's barrage was not heavy and there were gaps in it which enabled the Companies to get through with slight casualties. The fumes from the mine craters which were exploded at zero hour were the NAG'S NOSE were very noticeable. Our barrage was shocking slight on the right during the advance teams. Several casualties. All objectives were reached by the times laid down on arrival at the BLUE LINE a gap was found between the right of the Battalion and the 16" Division on our left, but touch was regained on arrival on the GREEN LINE.	
		7.20am	After the consolidation on the GREEN LINE about 3.0pm orders were received that the Battalion would move	

WAR DIARY
or
INTELLIGENCE SUMMARY.

(Erase heading not required.)

Army Form C. 2118.

Place	Date	Hour	Summary of Events and Information	Remarks and references to Appendices
		8.45 am	forward of the BLACK LINE to relieve a Battn. of 57 Bde who were to make a further advance. The Battn. therefore took up and continued the consolidation of this line. NV 9 of others were received that the Battalion should take over OIL TRENCH (part of the MAUVE LINE), but on arrival they were not required and the Battn was sent back to continue the consolidation of the BLUE LINE, and full NV in a state of Defence. Total casualties on 7" were as follows; 4 officers wounded (Capt. Saunders, 2LN Richards (RE's), 2 LN Morris E. (B ly) 2LN Wade AT (C ly)) = OR. Killed 23 Wounded 142 Missing 1. Prisoners taken 1 offr 219 OR. 12 Machine Guns and 2 Heavy Trench Mortars captured. Battalion remained on BLUE LINE	
	8			
	9		Battalion moved back to OB British line (BOIS CONFLUENT) in evening	
	10		Battalion took over line from a Battalion of 41st Division	

WAR DIARY
or
INTELLIGENCE SUMMARY.

Army Form C. 2118.

Place	Date	Hour	Summary of Events and Information	Remarks and references to Appendices
	14		in front of ROSE WOOD O16 (See Appendix B). A was front line was dug by the Battn while in the line. German shelling during this period was heavy - frequent barrages being put down on our line. Battalion was relieved in front line and by 9" R.W.F and moved to trenches near DAMMSTRASSE (HQ at DOME HOUSE) - 2 Coys remained in close support in BSTACLE SUPPORT	
	17		Bn relieved and moved to BOIS CARRE area - by 36" Division	
	18		Battalion moved to BIRR BARRACKS LOCRE	
	19		Battalion moved to camp near BAILLEUL.	
	30		Battalion did training from 19th to 30th	

Comdg 9th Service Bn The Welsh Regiment

Major

Army Form C. 2118.

WAR DIARY
or
INTELLIGENCE SUMMARY.
(Erase heading not required.)

Vol 2 3

9th (Sev) Battalion the Welch Regiment

War Diary

July 1917.

WAR DIARY
or
INTELLIGENCE SUMMARY.
(Erase heading not required.)

Army Form C. 2118.

Place	Date	Hour	Summary of Events and Information	Remarks and references to Appendices
	July 2nd		The Battalion moved to IRISH HOUSE - 58th Bde. being in Support & as from line.	
	9:		Battalion moved up in close support of 57th Bde; who were advancing their line. Bn in RIDGE DEFENCES HQrs in ONRAET WOOD	
	10:		Battalion relieved 8: Gloucesters Regt in Right Subsector of line	
	14:		Bn relieved in line by 9: Cheshire Regt and moved to ON RAET WOOD	
	15:		Battalion less D Coy, relieved by 7: H.D.R.L. and to BIRR BARRACKS EDGRE. D Coy relieves left Coy of 9: Cheshire Regt in line who had been evacuated.	
	19:	3.30am	D Coy counter-attached and driven out of JUNCTION BUILDINGS and re. took JUNCTION BLDGS with two platoons.	

WAR DIARY
or
INTELLIGENCE SUMMARY.
(Erase heading not required.)

Army Form C. 2118.

Place	Date	Hour	Summary of Events and Information	Remarks and references to Appendices
	19	4.15am	D. Coy were driven out of TONGTION BDGS Casualties 2/Lt SALMON 2/Lt V ROBERTS and 8 OR Killed 10 OR Wounded 6 OR Missing.	
	29		Battalion moves to Camp N.15.c.9.9 near KEMMEL	
	30		Bn moved into Bn Support area - RIDGE DEFENCES H.Q. COSTAVERNE WOOD in close support to 5" Br Whn were attacking on 31st.	

Lonsjany Lieut-Colonel
Comdg. 9th (S) Bn The Welsh Regt

WAR DIARY
or
INTELLIGENCE SUMMARY.

(Erase heading not required.)

9 Welsh Rg/ Army Form C. 2118.

Vol 24

24.L
2 whole

Place	Date	Hour	Summary of Events and Information	Remarks and references to Appendices
In line	Aug 1st 1917		The Battalion relieved 9. RWF in line in front of OOST AVERNE-	
			S.6. Bn. having attacked the day previous. Weather very bad &	
			trenches waterlogged. T/2Lt A/Capt T.W.C. Herbert & (O.C. B Coy) killed	
			while taking over the line and T/2Lt O.N. Nicholl - came killed -	
			2Lt. T.N. Roberts wounded.	
	2nd		Raining very heavily. T/2Lt A/Capt P.D. Bollans (O.C. A Coy) wounded	
			by sniper. Enemy very active with gas shells.	
Irish House	3rd		Batt. relieved by 9. Royal Welsh Fusiliers and moves to Camp	
			on IRISH HOUSE	
	5th		Batt. relieved 9. RWF in the line. Weather much better	
			and drier.	
	7th		19th Division relieved by 37th Division. Battalion relieved by	
			11th Warwicks and to Camp 3.1.D.7.6 near BAILLEUL. The Battalion	
			during the last two hours in the line has lost	
			3 officers killed 2 wounded and 5.O.R. casualties. The strength	
Bailleul			of the line was very low - all Companies under	

Army Form C. 2118.

WAR DIARY
or
INTELLIGENCE SUMMARY.
(Erase heading not required.)

Instructions regarding War Diaries and Intelligence Summaries are contained in F. S. Regs., Part II. and the Staff Manual respectively. Title pages will be prepared in manuscript.

Place	Date	Hour	Summary of Events and Information	Remarks and references to Appendices
BAYENGHEM	10"		comprised of two platoons only and the section strength was about 575. B" Battalion moved to BAYENGHEM - LES - SENINGHEM travelling by rail to WIZERNES. Company and individual training continues.	
FRONTIER Camp	27		Battalion moved to FRONTIER Camp between WESTOUTRE and BERTHEN. Battalion Company and Brigade training continues.	

J.H.S.N.
Major
Comdg 9: Welch Regt

WAR DIARY
or
INTELLIGENCE SUMMARY.

Army Form C. 2118.

58/19

Vol 25

War Diary Sept 1917
9 Welch Regt.

WAR DIARY
or
INTELLIGENCE SUMMARY.
(Erase heading not required.)

Army Form C. 2118.

Place	Date	Hour	Summary of Events and Information	Remarks and references to Appendices
	1-10		Battalion in FRONTIER Camp near WESTOUTRE	
	10		Battalion moved up to BOIS ENKRE	
	11		19° Division relieved 37° Division in line I (Sect. from YPRES–COMINES Canal to BELGIAN WOOD) 58° Bde on right and 57: on left. A comforte Bde in reserve commencing of 21 Col 9.05 hrs Bn. 9 Welch Regt took over the right Sector. Bn. confused as follows, 1 by of Cheshire Regt on L/W – 1 by 9 Welch in centre, 1 by 63 Welch on right – 1 by in EMBANKMENT. Each Battalion was later relieved on its attaching frontage.	
			Battalion was relieved by 13th KRR 37° Division and moves back to ROSSIGNOL Camp.	
	13		1 Coy moved up and took over Battalion attack frontage	

WAR DIARY
or
INTELLIGENCE SUMMARY.

Army Form C. 2118.

(Erase heading not required.)

Instructions regarding War Diaries and Intelligence Summaries are contained in F.S. Regs., Part II. and the Staff Manual respectively. Title pages will be prepared in manuscript.

Place	Date	Hour	Summary of Events and Information	Remarks and references to Appendices
	19		On night of 19/20 the Battalion moved to its assembly position. A very well ordered assembly was carried out with some difficulty. Major J.N.O. B. GODFREY being in command of the Battalion. Lt. Col GODFREY being attached to Brigade Headquarters.	Appendix 1
	20	3.40 am	The Battalion attacked. Heavy M.G. fire was encountered from HOLLEBEKE CHATEAU and from Sigurd O6 c 85.55. A Coy (Capt EN EDWARDS and C by Capt JD EVANS) SWB acts though being held up at Sigurd O6 B 60 30 by further through to final objective and established a post on the South of HESSIAN WOOD. On account of the mostly black smoke of HESSIAN WOOD N was scaled off and lain on West side of HESSIAN. The final line taken up by 58 BSe. is shown in black pencil on Appendix 2. Casualties were heavy mostly due to M.G. fire	Appendix 2

WAR DIARY
or
INTELLIGENCE SUMMARY.
(Erase heading not required.)

Army Form C. 2118.

Place	Date	Hour	Summary of Events and Information	Remarks and references to Appendices
	21		Following officers were killed: Major J.A. Gibbs DSO, Capt & 2/Lt Price Jones, 2/Lt Jukes, 2/Lt J.A. Jones. Died of wounds 2/Lt Griffith. 2/Lt More. Wounded Capt J.& T. Evans 6th SWB att'd. 9 Welch Regt Capt L.W. L'Suvens 2/Lt O.C. Smith, 2/Lt Rashus (OC D Cy) 2/Lt Gould 2/Lt Tonkin. Sixteen officers wear units action OR casualties were 35 killed 204 wounded 40 missing. Bn relieves in line by 7th MORL (56 Bde) & 6th ROYSLEVES Camp.	
			Bn moves to BOIS CONFLUENT in Bde in Divisional reserve.	
	29		Battalion took over line from Canal at Earl of Hessian Wood.	

Lieut. Col. Cross
9 Welch Regt

OPERATION ORDERS, No.25.   19/7/17.
BY LIEUT-COLONEL W. GODFREY. D.S.O.
COMDG. 9th BATTN. WELCH REGT.

___

ASSEMBLY.
　　　The Battalion will assemble for the attack on the night 19/20th Sept.

DRESS.
　　　Fighting order.

ROUTE.
　　　Coys will embus at N. 16. d. 2. 5. on KEMMEL - VIERSTRAAT Rd at 7 p.m. and debus at ESTAMINET CORNER, thence to the line by IN DE STERKTE Cross Rd, DOME HOUSE and ASSEMBLY TRACK. Distance of 100 yards between Platoons to be maintained.

BUSSES.
　　　Eight busses per company and one for Hd Qrs will be available.

ORDER OF MARCH.
　　　The 9th Welch Regt will be the first to embus in the following order:-
　　　　C.Coy., D.Coy., Composite Coy & Hd Qr Coy.
　　　(On debussing Coys will proceed direct to their positions)

KIT.
　　　Men are on no account to take off their kit whilst in the busses.

~~LEWIS GUNS.~~
　　　~~Lewis Guns will be at the Junction of OAF TRENCH and road at 9.15 p.m.~~

SILENCE.
　　　Attention is once again drawn to the necessity for strictest silence to be maintained during the assembly.

REPORT.
　　　Companies will report assembly complete by runner as quickly as possible when their men are in position.

LEWIS GUNS.
　　　Lewis Guns will be at the Junction of OAF TRENCH and the road at 9.15 p.m. O/C Coys will detail two Lewis Gunners per team to accompany the limbers. Lewis Guns and ammunition will be carried from the Junction of OAF TRENCH and road to the point where the ASSEMBLY TRACK cuts the EMBANKMENT, by the carrying party. At this point they will be handed over to Companies as they pass.

　　　　　　　(signed)　D.K. BOURNE.　Capt & Adjutant.
　　　　　　　　　　　　　　　　　　9th Battn. The Welch Regiment.

OPERATION ORDERS
BY LIEUT COLONEL W.GODFREY. D.S.O.
COMDG 9th BATTALION WELCH REGIMENT. 17/9/17.

D Coy

1. REFERENCE.
    HOLLEBEKE 1/10,000.

2. THE BATTALION FRONTAGE AND BOUNDARIES as on map issued to Companies.
    The 8th Bn Wiltshire Regt will be on our right, and the 9th Bn Cheshire Regt on our left.

3. ASSEMBLY.
    Four lines will be taped on the night before the attack. Sections will keep together round shell holes and the leading wave will only shake out into lines when the O.C. leading Companies consider the ground fit.
    All extension will be to the left.
    Strict silence and no lights or unnecessary talking is to be ensured. If the enemy knew of our assembly it would be fatal.

4. DISTRIBUTION & PLAN OF ATTACK.
    The attack will be carried out in four waves:-
    C.Coy on right, D.Coy on left forming 1st & 2nd wave.
    A.Coy on right, B.Coy on left forming 3rd & 4th wave.
    Waves will consist of 2 lines.
    The second wave of C and D.Coys must be prepared to detach men to mop up if they are passing likely places and the next wave is too far behind.
    The third wave will mop up to the final objective and when all the ground is cleared, withdraw to intermediate line.
    The fourth wave will stop in the intermediate line and will act as Battalion Reserve.
    The second wave will be on the look out to fill gaps and watch the flanks.
    O.C. A and B.Companies will be with their leading waves to direct mopping up. Special parties will be told off for certain likely places. The rest will mop at sight.
    The second wave will remain in sections in file as long as possible.
    The third wave will remain in sections in file in one line, each section with two scouts close to the second wave.
    The fourth wave will remain in sections in file in one line.
    Waves will start together to get clear of assembly position and will then open out to :-
            15 yards between lines.
            25 yards between waves.

5. DIRECTION.
    C and D.Companies will detail an Officer to watch the direction on right and left flank.
    True bearing of advance is 132° Variation is 12° West. All Compasses will therefore be set to march on 144°, unless their variation is exceptional.
    Right flank marches by left of OPAQUE WOOD and right of thick green undergrowth visible East of this WOOD.
    Left flank to the Gallows on the Hill at right of Copse, then to point 100 yards to left of far ridge of HESSIAN WOOD.
    Sections on each flank will dovetail with neighbouring Battalions.
    Intermediate line runs 100 yards North West of HESSIAN WOOD having a group of seven dug-outs in centre at O.6.b.7.1.

(2)

6. CONSOLIDATION.

The front and intermediate line will be consolidated by two lines of Posts each.

The lines of posts should be about 50 yards distance from each other and irregularly placed.

Immediately it is dark or the situation admits of it, the Battalion carrying party will bring forward wire and stakes and the whole front will be wired on the Battalion system, wire at least 40 yards from Posts.

7. MACHINE GUNS.

There will be a barrage starting with the Artillery Barrage. Two Guns will move on the left rear of 9th Cheshire Regt to position at P.1.a.6.7.

Two Guns will move in rear of 9th Welch Regt to spur near Intermediate line.

Both these sub-sections will cover the left flank if held up until defensive flanks can be formed, or will fill any gap.

Two Guns under O.C. 9th Welch Regt will advance in rear of left of first wave. They will take up the best position between intermediate and front line for covering the latter.

As these teams can only move slowly, second and subsequent waves will pass through them if necessary.

8. COUNTER ATTACK.

A counter attack must be expected.

Troops will hang on to all ground to be held and will use their rifles freely and immediately.

Counter attacks will be met by Unit Commanders in rear pushing up fresh troops without waiting for orders and before the enemy can reach our advance posts.

All ranks have got into a bad habit when they see an enemy of talking about it first. Shoot first and talk afterwards.

9. COMMUNICATION.

Brigade Visual Station ... O.5.b.5.5.
Brigade Forward Station... I.36.d.40.25.

On the 9th Welch Headquarters moving forward, a Brigade detachment will move to their command post laying two lines, one Artillery and one Infantry.

The 9th Welch Forward Command Post will be at O.6.b.85.60.

Pigeons. Two pigeons will go with each of the leading Companies.

After dark and after Zero hour, all tracks will be used as IN trenches. OAF and IMPERIAL Avenues as OUT trenches.

During assembly hour all routes will be used as IN trenches.

10. ARTILLERY.

Barrage as per map issued to Companies.

O.C. Companies will make as much use as possible of Forward Liasson Officers and will afford him every facility for sending messages.

When the barrage is pausing, plus 50 to plus 64, on our left, and also when it reaches the final objective, it will fire for 10 minutes a few smoke shells to show the Infantry where they have got to. Officers will follow the barrage closely with their watches.

11. STOKES MORTARS.

The two Guns attached to this Battalion will start in rear of the

(3)

11. **STOKES MORTARS.** Contd.
the/ third wave in the centre of each half Company. They will deal with any M.G. or S.P. holding up the advance, and take up position on the Intermediate Line.

12. **PATROLS.**
O.C. A and B. Companies. will each tell off a strong patrol from their rear two platoons to clear the ground when the barrage lifts to about 400 yards from our front line, to allow of this. They must make their way to the front and be ready to move out the moment the barrage lifts which will be one hour after plus 96. They will have one hour in which to clear the front under a protective barrage.

13. **DOCUMENTS.**
A special party under O.C. Scouts will search all dug-outs etc. Documents will be tied in bundles, put in sacks, and labelled as to locality.
N.C.O. will wear a "Brassard" "INTELLIGENCE" and will forward all documents immediately to Brigade Headquarters.

14. **PRISONERS.**
A special N.C.O. per Company will be told off to superintend escorts to Prisoners. If he has not sufficient slightly wounded men, he will get them from the nearest Officer. He will not allow prisoners to drift through our ranks but will collect them together.

15. **HOSTILE AEROPLANES.**
If any fly low over the troops in the assembly position, nobody must look up and all ranks will keep quite still.

16. **REORGANIZATION.**
The C.O. wishes to draw special attention to this. It is the most important point in the fight.
Section Commanders must on all occasions, and especially on getting to their objective, get their section together. No excuse can be taken, as without this consolidation is impossible and resistance to a counter attack very doubtful.

17. **FLAMMENWERFER.**
These may be met with but all ranks must realise *they only last* 5 seconds. Shoot the man who is working it if possible.

18. **S.O.S. SIGNALS.**
In use. Rifle Grenade Signal - Parachute - with three colours - Red over Green over Yellow.
First Change. Rifle Grenade Signal - Parachute - Light changing ~~if necessary~~ from White to Green.
Second Change. 1½ inch VERY LIGHT - Parachute - changing from ~~if necessary~~, White to Red.

19. **CARRYING PARTY.**
A carrying party under Sgt Richards of ~~No~~ 40 men will assemble at the Battalion Dump behind the Railway Line and on the first possible occasion will bring forward wire, stakes and French wire to front line.
The Battalion Carrying Party must be prepared during the fight to send forward Bombs or Ammunition if needed.

(4)

20. MAPS.
No Maps showing our own positions will be taken into the fight.

21. RUSES.
Cases have occurred of enemy shamming death. Any bunch of dead men should be tested in passing with the nearest handy instrument.
There is no such order as "RETIRE" and the man using it will be taken under immediate control by any means at hand.

22. FLAGS.
Flags will on no account be stuck in the ground.
Two will be carried by each platoon proceeding to furthest objective and displayed at intervals to help the Artillery.

R.E.

23. CONSTRUCTION OF STRONG POINTS.
The 82nd Field Coy, R.E. will construct a Strong Point on 58th Brigade Front at :-
          No 1 Post about O.6.b.8.9.
The Strong Point should be for a Garrison of one platoon and two Vickers Guns.
The Garrison will be detailed beforehand as under :-
    "O.C. A.Coy will detail this Garrison".
No 1 Post:- 9th Bn Welch Regt and one or two of the Machine Guns detailed to move forward to Intermediate Line when released from Barrage.
This Garrison will occupy the Strong Point as soon as reported ready for occupation by the R.E. Officer in charge.
O.C. 82nd Field Coy, R.E. will detail two parties with mobile charges to assist in the destruction of dug-outs beyond the final objective line. They will also be available if necessary to blow in the doors of any dug-outs which contain Germans and which cannot be entered. These parties will assemble with Battalion H.Q. of 9th Bn Welch Regt. and 9th Bn Cheshire Regt. They will move forward in rear of the last wave of the attack of the Battalions to which attached, keeping touch with the rear Company Commander of the Battalion.

24. REFERENCES TO TIME.
The words "Plus" or "Minus" will always be written.

25. HELMETS.
Helmets will not be covered but mud must be rubbed all over them before troops go into the line.

26. HEADQUARTERS.
Brigade ... ... O.36.b.9.8.
9th Bn. Welch Regt ... Dug-outs I.36.d.35.20., I.36.d.32.10.
6th Wilts Regt. ... O.6.a.4.7.,
9th Cheshire Regt. ... I.36.d.49.40.
9th R.W.Fusiliers. ... I.36.c.3.9.

Captain & Adjutant.
9th Bn Welch Regiment.

CONTACT PATROLS.

1. Aeroplanes for Contact Patrols will be R.E.8 type and will be specially marked by a Black Flap attached to the rear of each lower plane.

2. The Contact Patrol will fly over the line and call for flares at the following hours. Troops will also be prepared to put out flares at any other time if the Aeroplane calls for them.

   Zero plus 45 minutes.
   Zero plus 115 minutes.

3. Aeroplanes will call for flares and WATSON FANS by sounding a Klaxon Horn and firing a "VERY" white light, or by giving either of these two signals.

4. Red flares will be used. They should be lit in bunches of three each about 50 yards apart.
   WATSON FANS will be used in conjunction with flares. The Fans should be turned over every two seconds and not quicker. This signal will be made for periods of not less than two minutes at a time as the observer is sometimes in a position from which he cannot see the Fans.

5. CODE LETTERS FOR LIAISON
   BETWEEN INFANTRY AND AIRCRAFT.

58th Brigade	LI.
9/Cheshire Regt.	LIW.
9/R.W. Fusiliers	LIX.
9/Welch Regt.	LIY.
6/Wilts Regt.	LIZ.

   Captain & Adjt.
   9th Bn Welch Regiment.

17/9/17.

ADMINISTRATIVE ORDERS.
BY LIEUT COLONEL W.GODFREY. D.S.O.
COMDG 9th BATTALION WELCH REGT.   17/9/17.

1. **SURPLUS PERSONNEL.**
   Surplus Personnel will be accommodated at the 1st Line Transport, leaving the Battalion at noon two days before the Attack.

2. **MEDICAL.**
   Aid Post ...   I.36.c.2.0.   Railway Embankment.
                  Walking Wounded O.2.d.8.7. The Mound.

3. **PRISONERS.**
   Brigade Cage on track north of Buffs Bank.
   Escorts will not be more than 10% and will use overland tracks.
   Prisoners will not be searched.
   Looting is forbidden, but if a man tries to destroy papers they will be taken from him.
   Officers and N.C.Os will be kept separate.
   Receipts will be taken for all prisoners.

4. **AMMUNITION.**
   Brigade Dumps :-   OPAQUE WOOD   O.6.a.2.6.
                      IMPERFECT COPSE   I.36.d.35.10.

5. **R.E.**
   Same as Ammunition Dumps.

6. **STRAGGLERS POSTS.**
   O.4.a.7.9., and O.4.a.7.8.
   Collecting Station :-   O.2. central.

7. **RATIONS.**
   Battalion Dump will be in rear of Railway Embankment containing 200 tins of water and an issue of Iron Rations.
   No man is to use his Water Bottle before Zero hour.

8. **TROPHIES.**
   All articles claimed must be labelled and a claim submitted. Number and mark should be stated.

9. **DRESS.**
   As detailed at conference.
   C and D. Companies have Yellow patches on Haversacks.
   A and B. Companies carry two bombs per man.
   Sacks. Four to every man.
   S.A.A. 170 rounds per man.
   Bombers & Rifle Grenadiers, six each.
   Every man to have a tool, Proportion, 1 pick to 5 Shovels.

   The above does not apply to Runners, No. 1 & 2 Lewis Gunners, Signallers etc.

Captain & Adjutant.

OPERATION ORDERS (Continued)
BY LIEUT COLONEL W.GODFREY, D.S.O.
COMDG 9th BATTN WELCH REGIMENT.

1. The Brigade will assemble for Attack on night 6/7th

2. All movements to position of assembly will be by platoons at 100 yards distance. Troops will move in file.

3. **MARKERS.**
   Companies will arrange to have markers for each platoon in their assembly positions by 9-15 p.m. on the above night. These markers will be in position after dark to assist Companies in assembling.

4. The absolute necessity of strict silence during the march and after assembly is to be thoroughly impressed on all ranks. Any orders must be passed in a low tone of voice.

5. The greatest care must be taken that equipment does not rattle. Mess tins especially must be firmly fastened, and Bayonet Scabbards will be tied to entrenching tools.

6. No smoking, striking matches or flashing torches is to be allowed under any circumstances.

7. The latter portion of the night will be bright moonlight. It is therefor essential that every possible precaution be taken to prevent anything flashing. For this reason Bayonets will not be fixed until after zero and this must be done quietly.

8. **Y day.**
   Personnel of Battalion H.Q's, not required on march with unit will move to Battle H.Q. N.11.b.9.8. by 6 p.m.

9. Companies will report to Battalion Battle Headquarters, N.11.b.9.8., as soon as troops are in position and everything is ready.

OPERATION ORDERS (Continued)
BY LIEUT COLONEL W.GODFREY.
COMDG 9th BATTN WELCH REGT.

1. CORRECTIONS.
   Para. 11. lines 5, 6 and 7 commencing RED, BLUE, GREEN add at end of each line, "Before this hour."
   Para. 13. line 2, for "O.13.b.3.4." read " O.13.b.5.2."

2. COMMUNICATION.

   Battalion will use Watson Fans beside Green Flares to show the position of Front Line. They will be moved from side to side showing white face for 3 seconds at a time.

3. TANKS.
   (1) One section of Tanks of "A" Battalion, 2nd Brigade, Heavy Branch, M.G.Corps, (2 male and 2 female) will co-operate in the attack on the left flank of the Division.
   They will start on Zero day so as to arrive on the BLUE LINE about CATTEAU FARM at the time the Infantry advance from the BLUE LINE, viz., Zero plus 3.40 and will advance one pair against OBTUSE KEEP, ONRAET FARM and by West of ONRAET WOOD to the ESTAMINET, one pair by OBTUSE CRESCENT - EVAN'S FARM to BONDULLE FARM.

   (2) All ranks should be warned that they should on no account wait for Tanks, and that the action of the Tanks is entirely supplementary to the Infantry assault, and are not to be relied upon.

AMENDMENT TO OPERATION ORDERS.
BY LIEUT COLONEL W. GODFREY. D.S.O.
COMDG 9th BATTN WELCH REGIMENT.   19/9/17.

Para. 12.
 PATROLS.
    The barrage will lift at Zero plus 2 hours 30 minutes to allow patrols to clear the front.
    The protective barrage will cease at Zero plus 3½ hours 30 minutes.

Para. 23.
 R.E.
    R.E. with mobile charges will accompany patrols to clear the front at Zero plus 2 hours 30 minutes.

SYNCHRONISATION OF WATCHES.
    Watches will be synchronised today at Brigade Headquarters at 4 p.m. and 10 p.m.
    2nd Lieut. Thompson will be responsible for this synchronisation.

[signature]
Capt. & Adjt.
9th Bn Welch Regt.

HOLLEBEKE

GERMAN TRENCHES CORRECTED TO 25·9·17 Part of Sheet 28.

EDITION 2.A

NOTE. A footwater canal exists along the western side of the canal from D. 20 to 7.4 northward 10, 12 & 16 N.O.S. 9.1, and is conducted to tunnels at three points indicated. Vide also HOUTHEM Sheet.

Scale 1:10,000

WAR DIARY
or
INTELLIGENCE SUMMARY.

9th (S) Bn: The Welch Regiment

War Diary

October 1917

WAR DIARY
or
INTELLIGENCE SUMMARY.
(Erase heading not required.)

Army Form C. 2118.

Instructions regarding War Diaries and Intelligence Summaries are contained in F. S. Regs., Part II. and the Staff Manual respectively. Title pages will be prepared in manuscript.

Place	Date	Hour	Summary of Events and Information	Remarks and references to Appendices
	October 1-2		Battalion in line from Canal to East of HESSIAN WOOD	
	3		Bn: relieved by 6th Welsh. "A" & "D" Coys moved to BOIS CONFIDENT (O.I.C.) "B.C." H.Q. — SPOIL BANK.	
	6		In Support as above	
	7		Bn. Relieved 6 Welsh in the Right Sub Sector of the line:- "D" Coy on left "C" in centre "A" on Right "B" in the EMBANKMENT each having a platoon in the Forward Posts.	
	10		In line as above	
	11		Bn. relieved by 8th N Staffs and moved to BEAVER CAMP	
	12-18		Bn: Training at BEAVER CAMP	
	11		Lieut Col. L.C. Guefrey 150th to England for 6 months rest. Major E.F. King M.C. (9th Welsh Regt) assumes command.	

T 2134. Wt. W708—776. 50000. 4/15. Sir J. C. & S.

WAR DIARY
or
INTELLIGENCE SUMMARY.
(Erase heading not required.)

Army Form C. 2118.

Place	Date	Hour	Summary of Events and Information	Remarks and references to Appendices

	19		Bn: relieved the 8th GLOUCESTER Regt in the Right Sub-Sector of line
			 Dispositions:
			      B. — Left
			      D. — Centre
			      A. — Right
			      C. — Reserve	

	20		Bn: awarded following decorations for gallantry etc in attack on HESSIAN WOOD on September 20. T/Lieut A Capt D.K. BOURNE } T/ " " R.J. WILLIAMS } D.S.O T/Capt. I.T EVANS — 5th Suff.B. attd 9. Wel. } T/Capt A.W Young: RAMC attd 9 Wel } M.C. T/2 Lieut H.T. Horsfall attd 58.TMB }	

Army Form C. 2118.

WAR DIARY
or
INTELLIGENCE SUMMARY.
(Erase heading not required.)

Instructions regarding War Diaries and Intelligence Summaries are contained in F. S. Regs., Part II. and the Staff Manual respectively. Title pages will be prepared in manuscript.

Place	Date	Hour	Summary of Events and Information	Remarks and references to Appendices
	19		33690 C.S.M. J.D. MORRIS 16757 L.Cpl T.J. GREEN 15625 Pte H. DAVIES awd 5th TMB	D.C.M.
			19 Military heads were also awarded to the Battalion	
	23		Bn. Relieved in the line by 6" Welch 'A'. B. C. & H.Q. to SPOIL BANK. D Coy GASPERS CLIFF. In Support	
	27		Bn relieved by 7th S. LANCS and moved to camp at O.1.A.6.3 [MOATED GRANGE]	
	28		ditto	
	29		"	
	30		"	
	31			

C.J. King Major
Commdg. 9th Welch Regt.

Army Form C. 2118.

WAR DIARY
or
INTELLIGENCE SUMMARY.
(Erase heading not required.)

9 Welsh R¹
Vol 27

Instructions regarding War Diaries and Intelligence Summaries are contained in F. S. Regs., Part II. and the Staff Manual respectively. Title pages will be prepared in manuscript.

Place	Date	Hour	Summary of Events and Information	Remarks and references to Appendices
	Nov 1917			
	1/3		Battalion at Camp at O.1.A.6.3 (Goats Grange)	
	4		moved to Camp at N.19.d.4.5 (Kemmel Shelters)	
	5/7		training at above	
	8		moved by road & billets in Brazile area	
	9/10		training at Brazile	
	11		moved by road to billets in Lynde area	
	12/28		training in Lynde area	
	29		proceeded by road to Connette area at Pont du Hem	
			training	
	29		Total Ribbons issues:— by O.i.C Division at Ellinghem	
			2 Officers (Bell & Bourn D.S.O)	
			& Lapointe (M.C)	
			14 OR	

Robt Starkey Lt
Lieut. Colonel
Comdg 9th (Ser.) Bn. THE WELCH REGt.

Headquarters.
    58th Brigade.

Herewith War Diary for December 1917.

                [signature]
                Capt for. Major.
                Comdg 9th Bn. Welch Regt.

31/12/17.
   A.48

WAR DIARY
or
INTELLIGENCE SUMMARY.
(Erase heading not required.)

Army Form C. 2118.

Vol 28

9th (S) Bn The Welch Regt

War Diary

December 1914

Army Form C. 2118.

WAR DIARY
or
INTELLIGENCE SUMMARY.
(Erase heading not required.)

Instructions regarding War Diaries and Intelligence Summaries are contained in F. S. Regs., Part II. and the Staff Manual respectively. Title pages will be prepared in manuscript.

Place	Date	Hour	Summary of Events and Information	Remarks and references to Appendices
	23		Batn. under canvas and in dug-outs in HAVINCOURT WOOD	
	24		" "	
	25		" moves to the Hindenburg Line	
	26		" in HINDENBURG LINE	
	27		" "	
	28		" move to billets in RIBECOURT	
	29		" "	
	30			
	31			

Lansdale Hammell MAJOR.
COMDG
9TH (S) BN THE WELCH REGT.

Army Form C. 2118.

WAR DIARY
or
INTELLIGENCE SUMMARY.
(Erase heading not required.)

9th (Service) Bn. The Welch Regt

War Diary

January. 1918

Army Form C. 2118

WAR DIARY
or
INTELLIGENCE SUMMARY
(Erase heading not required.)

Instructions regarding War Diaries and Intelligence Summaries are contained in F. S. Regs., Part II. and the Staff Manual respectively. Title Pages will be prepared in manuscript.

January.

Place	Date	Hour	Summary of Events and Information	Remarks and references to Appendices
Ribecourt	1	nept 9.	Batln in Ribecourt Ribecourt	
	2/3	"	1 Company takes over from 8th Gloucester Regt (57 Infy Bde)	
	3/4	"	3 Companies relieve 6th Wilts Regt	
	4/5	"	Relieved by 2/4th Bn. London Regt and move back to left sub-sector Intermediate Line	
	5/6	"	Take over left sub sector relieving 8th Bn Gloucester Regt	
	7	"	Bn HQ move into the Quarters of a Company of the 9th Cheshire in FOSS AVENUE.	
	13	"	Relieved & move into Intermediate Line taking over from 4th R. Lancs	
	14/14	"	Relieve 6th Wilts in left sub sector	
	18	"	Relieved by 9th Bn. L.N. Lancs Regt and move to HAWES CAMP West Havrincourt Wood	
	19/23	"	Stationed in HAWES CAMP WEST	
	24	2.PM	Move into Trenches ABay left, DBay Centre, & CBay Right & BBay Support. The Trench System in force and a Battn Rear Echelon formed and stationed at the Transport Lines to deal with "A" Work, Returns, ACMs &c.	
	28		Batln Relieved and move into Intermediate Line	
	29/30/31		" " Intermediate Line	

C.J.P. Simmons
Capt for
Lt Colonel
Comdg 9th (S) Bn. The Welch Regt

Army Form C.

Vol 30

WAR DIARY
or
INTELLIGENCE SUMMARY.

(Erase heading not required.)

9th (S) Bn. The Welsh Regt.

FEBRUARY
1918

Place	Date	Hour	Summary of Events and Information	Remarks and references to Appendices

Army Form C. 2118

WAR DIARY
or
INTELLIGENCE SUMMARY
(Erase heading not required.)

Instructions regarding War Diaries and Intelligence Summaries are contained in F. S. Regs., Part II. and the Staff Manual respectively. Title Pages will be prepared in manuscript.

Place	Date	Hour	Summary of Events and Information	Remarks and references to Appendices
In the field.	1/2/18 5/2/18		Relieve 8th North Staffordshire Regt in Reserve Sub Sector of Right Sector. Div Front Relieved by 11th KSLI and moved to Pioneer Camp. Nr LECHELLE.	
	6/2/18	2. PM	Move from PIONEER CAMP to GRAZING CAMP.	
	8/2/18		March off at 3 PM and relieve 1/4 S. LANCS in Intermediate Line	
	12/2/18		Relieve 11th KSLI in Centre Sector of Right Sub sector	
	14/2/18		Relieved by HOOD Battn 63rd Division. E Coy in Support relieved by DRAKE Bn	
			ENTRAIN at TRESCAULT for RUEGUIGNY.	
	15/22		Carry out training & Shots according to Programme at "A" Camp Rocquigny.	
	23/24	2 PM	March to Phipps Camp Nr. HARINCOURT.	
	24/26		Carry out training + Shots according to Programme at PHIPPS CAMP	
	27	9.35 AM	Practice Y Corps 2nd Defence Scheme	
	28		Usual training at PHIPPS CAMP.	

E Lawrence Capt
Lt Col
Comdg
9TH (S) BN THE WELCH REGIMENT.

VOL 31

19th Division
Brigade
58th Battalion.

WAR
DIARY

9th BATTALION

THE WELCH REGIMENT

MARCH 1918

Report on Operations attached.

Army Form C. 2118.

WAR DIARY
INTELLIGENCE SUMMARY.
(Erase heading not required.)

19th (S) Bn The Welch Regt

MARCH 1918

Place	Date	Hour	Summary of Events and Information	Remarks and references to Appendices

WAR DIARY
or
INTELLIGENCE SUMMARY
(Erase heading not required.)

Army Form C. 2118

Place	Date	Hour	Summary of Events and Information	Remarks and references to Appendices
	1/3/18 To 20/3/18		(Included St Davids Day) Carry out training & sports according to programme in PHIPPS CAMP Nr. HAPLINCOURT	
	21/3/18 To 26/3/18		See Special Diary Sheets 1–3 attached	
	27/3/18		Commence to re-organise at BAYENCOURT. Start at 9 AM and march to TAMACHON arriving at 1·30 PM	
	28/3/18		In billets at TAMACHON. Start at 2 AM 30/3/18 and march to CANDAS arriving at 8·AM. Entrain 3·15 PM arrive at CAESTRE at 11·PM proceeding by busses to LOCHRE.	
	29d to 30.			
	31st		Continue Re-organisation at DONCASTER HUTS. LOCHRE.	

M.Davis
Capt & Major Comdg
9th(S) Bn The Welch Regiment

Headquarters
    58th Inf. Bde.

Herewith an account of the
actions of the Battalion between
21st + 27th March —
Reference your   B.M. 311 of 31/3/18

A.9.
3/4/18.

J.D.Davies Capt & Adjt
for Major Commanding
9th "B." The Welch Regt

9th Batt: The Welch Regt

Diary from 21st March to 27th March 1918

March 21st — The 9th B: Welch Regt was billetted in PHIPPS CAMP, BERTINCOURT on the morning of March 21st, and at 4.45 a/m "stood-to" in camp because of an intense hostile barrage on the British front-line.

Orders to move to assembly positions in GAIKA COPSE arrived at 10 a/m, and the move itself was completed by 11.15 a/m. During this time the enemy shelled the surroundings intensely with heavy guns, but no casualties were sustained. The battalion remained in these positions until 2 p/m when a forward move to battle positions on the line extending from J.28.a.3.1 to J.28.b.5.1 was ordered. One Company was despatched immediately to establish battle-outposts forward of this line to cover the movement of the remainder of the batt: which reached the new position by 5 p/m. At 11 p/m D Coy was advanced to the HERMIES SWITCH to reinforce the 51st Division, and had just established themselves there when the whole battalion side-stepped to new Assembly positions in I 29. This move was completed by

March 22nd — 5 a/m on the 22nd March.

At 11⁰⁰ʰʳ the battalion moved forward to a position in Brigade reserve for the defence of BEAUGNY. Here the dispositions were, D Company in the village, A, B and C Companies occupying a continuous line extending from I 15 d. through I 16 a. and d. as far as the main CAMBRAI - BAPAUME Road, [which positions were maintained until 4ᵖᵐ]. At 6.30ᵖ, B and C Companies were ordered to make an attack [with] in co-operation with tanks, the objective being the road through I 4 c, and the purpose to connect the left of the Brigade with the 41ˢᵗ Division. Owing to a threatened enemy attack on the centre of the Brigade however, these Companies were not sent forward and the battalion remained in readiness to deliver a counter-attack. The position remained intact, the front-line battalions having dealt effectively with the enemy's repeated attacks, until 10⁰⁰ᵃᵐ on the 23ʳᵈ March. During the morning of the 23ʳᵈ, the enemy continued to launch attacks on our front-line. Troops south of the CAMBRAI-BAPAUME road began to fall back, and the enemy having secured LEBOUQUIÈRE was advancing strongly through I 23.c. at 12.30ᵖᵐ.

March 23ʳᵈ

(3)

In the meantime D Company had assumed a position in the road running through I 22 c and d, and C Company was instructed to strengthen the right flank. This Company took up a line on the right of and in prolongation with D Company, and connected with the K.O.S.L.I. whose position was the GREEN LINE in I 28.a. The enemy repeatedly attacked these positions in the afternoon without success. At 4-30 p.m. he attacked across the main-road and penetrated our line in I 16 d and c, and gaining a footing in the Northern edge of the village by 5 p.m. In accordance with instructions, the battalion was withdrawn in perfect order to the GREEN LINE and by 12 midnight was established in its new position, two Companies in front in I 20 b. and two Companies in the immediate rear as supports.

Mar. 24th During the morning of the 24th March an enemy relief was observed in progress in I 22 b. on the Southern side of the main CAMBRAI - BAPAUME road. At 11 a.m. orders were received indicating the line of retirement should a withdrawal become necessary by reason of the defection of the right flank. At 2 p.m. a withdrawal became imperative, the troops on the right having fallen away, and this was effected under covering fire from the supporting battalion, in an orderly manner. The next position adopted was astride the main road in I 28 c and this was held until 2ᵃᵐ on the 25ᵗʰ March when in consequence of the units on the right and left having withdrawn long previously and the fact that the Division had taken up positions in I 31 c and d, the Batt: fell back on this main line of defence, which was reached by 3-15 %ₘ, and where the men dug themselves in in a position facing East. The Division on the right was aligned along the BAPAUME – ALBERT Road, facing South East where the enemy's main attack was being delivered This Division withdrew through our line and thereby made it necessary for us to bend back the right along the ridge running through H. 31.C. and C. 36.d, where the line was continued Westwards by the S.W.B. who were in support. From 9 %ₘ to 12 noon there was a fierce combat in which our troops by a development of rifle-fire broke down every attempt on the part of the enemy to advance. By this time, hostile M.Gs had worked into positions in rear of our left and harrassed our line. When

March 25ᵗʰ

(5)

the troops on the right also withdrew, there was only one course of action to prevent our being cut off altogether. Excellent and skilful rearguard actions and well-controlled covering fire enabled us to attain the ridge in C.29 in good order and with very few casualties. This was the next main line of defence and was occupied by the 61st, parts of the 19th, and 51st Divisions. The right flank continued to yield under very heavy pressure. By this time the battalion was very scattered and numbered hardly more than 25, and with these men strong points were held in LOUPART WOOD which were held for a considerable period, and only abandoned when the troops on the right and left fell back. Another stand was made on the high ground in C.33. where the remainder of the Division was assembled. Here the battle swayed and the enemy more or less was held. At 11th the whole 26th Naval. Division was withdrawn to a position around PUSIEUX-AU-MONT, and at 2% a further withdrawal to HÉBUTERNE was ordered, and here a thorough reorganisation of battalions was effected, and preparations made to defend the village. The troops were rested for a few hours.

(6)

At 9.30% it was reported that the enemy had gained a footing in the village. Fighting patrols were at once pushed up the village and were met by a good deal of sniping. The remainder of the battalion took up a position in HQ a and from here several fighting patrols and ~~sweeping~~ mopping-up parties were sent through the village. There was a good deal of indiscriminate fighting but eventually the village was cleared, four prisoners and a M.G. taken, and strong posts established on the S.E. edge of the village ensuring our possession of it. At 10ᵗʰ the Battⁿ was relieved by a unit of an Australian Division and withdrew to rest-billets in BAYENCOURT.

10ᵖ/m 2/4/18.

H Lloyd Williams
Major
9ᵗʰ Welch Regᵗ

58th Brigade.
19th Division.

1/9th BATTALION

THE WELCH REGIMENT

APRIL 1918.

Report on Operations attached.

Army Form C. 2118.

WAR DIARY
or
INTELLIGENCE SUMMARY.
(Erase heading not required.)

9 Welch

Place	Date	Hour	Summary of Events and Information	Remarks and references to Appendices
LOCRE.	April 1st.		Reorganising at DONCASTER HUTS.	
	2nd.		Move to FUSILIER CAMP near NEUVE EGLISE and continue training and reorganising.	
	3rd) to 9th)		Training and reorganising.	
	10th to 20th		Carry out operations as per attached history. Lieut-Col. H.L. Jones, D.S.O. takes over command of the Battalion.	
	21st		Move to Paddington Camp, near PROVEN for training and reorganisation.	
	22nd) to 24th)		Training.	
	25th		Provide working party (400) to construct line of defence between the POPERINGHE - BUSSEBOOM Road.	
	26th	4.am	Moved to a camp near BUSSEBOOM.	
	27th	7.pm	Moved up to dig VLAMENTINGHE - HALLEBAST Line. Received message to man the line.	
	28th) to 29th)		Remained in VLAMENTINGHE - HALLEBAST Line as counter-attacking battalion to 21st Division.	
	30th	10.pm	Relieved the 8th Leicesters (21st Div) in front line (G.H.Q. Line).	

(sd) H.L. JONES, Lieut-Colonel
Commanding 58th Infantry Brigade.

58th Infantry Bde.

Herewith account of operations
from 10th – 28th April 1918.
This account has been prepared
by Major Lloyd Williams R.W.F.

H. G. Frum W Ld
9th Welsh Regt.

24/4/18

B 13

9th (S) Bn The Welch Regiment

Operations from 10th - 20th April 1918

April 10th 1918. Battalion in Brigade Reserve in ONRAET WOOD NORTH HOUSE ZERO HOUSE. Battalion Hd Qrs in ONRAET FARM.

8.30 a.m. At 8.30 a.m. verbal orders arrived from G.O.C Brigade to occupy cutting in O.19 c & d with two Companies (C & D) and prevent a threatened enemy attack on WYTSCHAETE from the MESSINES direction.

"A" Company was detailed to fill up gaps in the front line which was being held by 6th S.W.B's and Warwicks and ran approximately through GUN F^m BAY F^m and PICK HOUSE.

All these positions were subjected to the most intense shelling throughout the day and the positions of the front line varied at different hours.

3 pm At 3 pm in consequence of a strong attack on the Posts in RAVINE WOOD B Coy was ordered to reinforce the left of the Brigade front and occupied posts

9 pm in PHEASANT WOOD. By 9 pm these Companies with other troops in the vicinity withdrew under orders of the 9th Division to the DAMSTRAASE where it came under the command of the 26th Brigade. Here it assisted materially in repelling a hostile

April 11th attack on the morning of the 11th April and in reoccupying posts in PHEASANT WOOD.

The positions of all the Companies remained
April 12th unchanged throughout the 11th & 12th April.

9 pm At 9 pm the whole Battalion was taken out

and reassembled in JAMAICA CAMP LA CLYTTE where the task of reorganisation was commenced.

April 13th
10 a.m. At 10 a.m. on April 13th, the Battalion was ordered to assemble on the right of the LA CLYTTE - KEMMEL ROAD
3 p.m. and at 3 p.m. a move was made via KEMMEL and LINDENHOEK to the SPY FARM - SPANBROEKMOLEN ridge where new lines were dug. This line it was ordered, had to be held at all costs. Three Companies less two platoons occupied a line organised in depth which ran generally along N.28.d.4.4 N.29.c.6.5, N.29.d.8.8 thence along road to N.30.a.2.7. Two Companies less two platoons were reserved for counter-attack purposes in N.23.c. and d.

14th and 15th April
Such was the position until the night 14th/15th April when B Company were sent to the Welsh and occupied positions as follows :- One platoon in close support to front line at N.30.c.2.2. Two platoons for counter attack on SPANBROEKMOLEN at N.35.c.2.6. One platoon in front at N.36.c.1.4. "C" Coy S.W.B. was attached to the G.O. Welsh and occupied positions in support in N.28.b. subsequently reinforcing the main line held by the Welsh with two platoons.

During the night, the Brigade on the right was compelled to withdraw its line, the location of
April 15th which was obscure throughout the day. This necessitated a bending of the right of B.Company which endeavoured to conform.
In the meantime, the SPY FARM - SPANBROEKMOLEN line was subjected to frequent and intense

hostile bombardments and particularly on the
part adjacent to SPANBROEKMOLEN

During the night 15th/16th April, a reorganisation
of the line took place and with the remainder of
the Welch, No 5 platoon of the Welch was withdrawn
from its forward position and thickened the
garrisons situated on the W. and S. of SPANBROEKMOLEN.

April 16th. At 8.30 a.m. on the 16th inst it was realised that
the enemy had gained a footing on the N.E. lip
of SPANBROEKMOLEN and harrassed D & B Companies
with Machine Guns and Trench Mortars from this
commanding position. It became necessary to
bend back the left of our line which by 2 p.m. was
as follows :- N.29.d.3.8. N.29.d.8.8. thence
along the road and northwards to N.29.b.7.6.
The two platoons of B. Company at N.30.c.2.6.
were withdrawn to this line.

In immediate support was C. Company which
took up a position around N.29.b.1.1.

This line remained intact throughout the rest
of the period despite very heavy casualties from
Shell fire, Machine Guns & Trench Mortars.

April 17th. Throughout the day April 17th, the enemy
dribbled up small numbers and from REGENT
STREET DUGOUTS and other unknown positions
in the STUIVERBECK Valley caused much trouble
with Machine Guns and Trench Mortars. Our
own active reply with Machine Guns and Rifles
very quickly suppressed this trouble and an

absolute mastery obtained.

4 pm At 4 pm a Battalion of the 22nd French Regt carried out a valiant attack on the VIERSTRAAT SWITCH under cover of a barrage accurately placed on our support line. The actual British front line being subsequently reached, another attempt to attack and retake SPANBROEKMOLEN was made with less success and equal damage. At 10 pm the Battalion, less C Company in support, was relieved in the front line by the Welch and took up positions in Reserve in N.28 d and N.22 d.

April 18th Nothing of importance more than heavy hostile bombardments on the front line, reserve lines and Battalion Hd Qrs (PARRAIN FARM) at 4 am, 5 am, 9 am, 10 am, 2.30 pm, 6 pm occurred subsequently on our front.

On the night 18th-19th April the Battalion had to endure an unrehearsed relief by the 22nd French Regt, a relief which was complete by 4 a m on the 19th inst.

The Battalion moved into billets in the POPERINGHE area in L.35.

H. D. Jones Lieut-Colonel
Comdg 9th (S) Bn Welch Regt

24/4/18.

9 West Regt

War Diary
or
Intelligence Summary

For the Month of May 1918

Vol 3 B

Place	Date	Hour	Summary of Events or Information	Remarks
In the Line	1-5-18 to 10-5-18		The Battalion in the positions vacated by The 8th Leicesters on the 30th of April (E.H.Q.I Line) and remained until the 10th inst when they were relieved by the 8th North Staffords. The relieve taking place during the night May 10th/11th. Each platoon on being relieved proceeded via, Ration Dump – Belgium Battery to the entraining station at Pioneer Junction H16.c.6.a. Guides were met at the detraining point who led the Battalion to Camp near Poperinghe.	
Camp	11-5-18			
"	12-5-18	9.45am	The Battalion & Transport proceeded by March Route ((Watou Herzeele Wylder)) to Wylder	
Wylder	13-5-18 to 17-5-18		Two Officers Capt H.B Saunders M.c. & Lt Robb the former from England and the latter from Hosp rejoined the Battalion, also a draft of 45 O.R.. At 6 P.M Lt.H. Evans proceeded to Rotronck for Gas Course.	
"	18-5-18	11.30am	Entrained at Nutheart Rispoorle. the Battalion travelled via Hayelles. Ponthore Chalons Thierry to railhead outside Chalons and detrained 6.30pm then marched the Village of St Germain La Ville	
St Germain to Ville	19-5-18 to 28-5-18		and were billeted there until the 28-5-18 Here the Battalion carried out a Training Programme whose classes were formed for instruction in the use of French Grenades and Bombs, under a Bombing Sergeant and two other Ranks belonging to the French Army	
			Operations from 28th May to 31st May – see attached	

N.R. Jones
Lieut Colonel

9th (S) Bn THE WELCH REGIMENT.

Operations from 29th May - 31st May, 1918.

Tuesday 28th May.   The Battalion embussed at 11.0.p.m. at ST. GERMAIN - LA - VILLE debussed at Cross Roads S.E. of Y in CHAMBRECY at 4.0.a.m. 29th May.

Wednesday 29th May.   Marched to billets in BLIGNY. At 8.0.a.m. Battalion moved up into support of 9th Bn R.W.Fusiliers about TRAMERY. The 9th Bn R.W.Fusiliers were holding a line from FAVEROLLES to COEMY. The Battalion was disposed as follows - 3 companies holding the line from the C of COEMY to the Y of TRAMERY touch on the left being maintained with 57th Inf. Bde. (8th Gloucester Regt) and with French troops on the right (6th Tirailleurs), one company in reserve in field just West of TRAMERY Village. These positions were held for this day. The Companies were fairly heavily shelled while taking up these positions but sustained but few casualties.

Thursday 30th May.   In the early morning the 9th Bn R.W.Fusiliers were ordered to withdraw their line through the 9th Bn Welch Regiment - The Battalion thus becoming front line troops at about 8.30.a.m. The French troops on the right then withdrew and took up a position along the TRAMERY - TREILIN Road. The right flank of the battalion then became exposed. The reserve company was ordered to fill the gap between the right of the battalion and 2nd Bn Wiltshire Regt. who were holding the BOULEUSE SPUR. This was effected about 10.30.a.m. The withdrawal of the 9th Bn R.W.Fusiliers had caused a certain amount of confusion and distrust to the Battalions on our flanks. But after consultation with the French Regimental Commanders to whom the situation was explained the position seemed to be satisfactory. Reports were received from the Left Company that the 57th Inf. Bde. were being heavily attacked and were falling back. The Left Company (B Company) was ordered to form a defensive flank which it did and reported that its position was safe at 10.30.a.m. About 11.0.a.m. orders were received from Bde. H.Q. for a withdrawal to a line in front of POILLY owing to the left of the Division front having given way. Orders were issued to all Companies to withdraw at 11.15.a.m. but by this time the left company wase engaged in hand to hand fighting and the enemy had worked his way behind Battalion H.Q. and it was only possible to effect the withdrawal of the right company ("C" Coy.). This Company then fell back and took up a line just in front of POILLY but verbal orders were received to withdraw to a line N.W? of SARCY which was being held by the 9th Bn Cheshire Regiment. This was done and the remnants of the battalion came under the orders of O.C., 9th Bn Cheshire Regiment.

                                                                                       Lieutenant Colonel

                                             Commanding 9th Bn The Welch Regiment.

15.6.18.

9A 34

WAR DIARY
OR
INTELLIGENCE SUMMARY

8th (SER.) BN. THE WELCH REGT.

Place	Date	Hour	Summary of Events or Information
	1/6/18		Diary of the share taken by the Battalion in the operations between June 1st 1918 and June 8th 1918.

At midday June 1st the 58th Inf. Bde. was disposed as follows. 2nd Wilts Regt. was holding a line running East to West on the high ground immediately North of CHAMBRECY [A.15.20 x A.12.85 A.21.6.10 x A.22.80]. The remaining units of the 58th Bde. were formed up on some large Company under the command of Major Lloyd Williams D.S.O. M.C. and were holding a line along the Bligny–CHAMBRECY road between the points A.16.40 x A.22.75 and A.15.73 x A.22.20. This Company also held some posts in advance of the wood, as follows:— (A) One platoon of the 9th Welch under 2/Lt J.E. Williams echeloned in rear of the 2nd Wiltshire Regt. 16 maintaining Liason with the French troops on Left. This platoon was entrenched at A.16.74 x A.22.46 x.   (b) One platoon of the 9th R.W.F. maintaining three posts at the following points. ⊙ A.16.15 x A.23.33.   (a) In the Farm. A.15.84 x A.23.05 x.   The 9th Cheshire Regt. were on their right flank of the 58th Brigade. At 4.0pm. under covering fire from the Montagne de Bligny the 2nd Wiltshires withdrew to a position along the western edge of the BOIS. DES. ECLISSES to conform with the French on their Left.   The remainder of the 58th Bde have changed direction half-left to take up a line just below the crest on the forward Western Slope of the Montagne De Bligny with the 9th Cheshires on the right. This Line was however heavily shelled, and at night (June 1st/2nd) the following reorganisation was carried out. The 9th Cheshires Regt, 9th R.W.F. 9th Welch and 58th Brigade T.M.B. were formed into one Battalion under the command of Major Lloyd Williams D.S.O. M.C. of the 9th R.W.F. and were known as the 9th Cheshires and came under the orders of the G.O.C. 50th Bde.   This Battalion (9th Cheshires) then took up a Line running as follows A.16.60 to the N of MONTAGNE then along the Western edges of the woods on the Western slope of the MONTAGNE DE BLIGNY to point 166.7. on the BLIGNY – CHAMBRECY road. |
| | 2/6/18 | | The day of June 2nd was quiet and during the afternoon further re-organisation was carried out. The 58th Composite Battn. under Lt. Col. Ralson 2nd Wilts, was formed, comprising three Coys:— 2nd Wilts Coy (Lt Melons) 9th R.W.F. (Capt. Fitzsimmons.) 9th Welch Coy (Capt. Saunders.) The 58th Bn was then disposed as follows:— B.H.Q at point 219.0 at the north edge of the BOIS. DES. ECLISSES. 2nd Wilts Coy from point 166.7 on BLIGNY–CHAMBRECY road, to the south along Western edge of BOIS. DES. ECLISSES. 9th R.W.F. Coy H.Q at point 181.8 on BLIGNY–CHAMBRECY road. 1 platoon in posts, extending as follows:— From S.W edge of wood, ½ inch. S.W. of ¼ m. MONTAGNE DE BLIGNY along forward slope 15 point 166.7 on the BLIGNY–CHAMBRECY road. 1 Platoon in Reserve in copse by the +7 of point 181.7. 9th Welch Coy H Q at point 181.8 on BLIGNY–CHAMBRECY road. 1 platoon holding a front line of 6 posts, as follows;- No1. N.E corner of wood, ¼ west of 1st in MONTAGNE DE BLIGNY.   No.2. N.W. Corner of above wood, This was a L.G. post.   No.3. In the centre of Western edge of same wood.   No.4. S.W. corner of same wood.   No.5. At point A15.10 x A.23.0 on forward slope concealed in copse between the two woods on Western slope.   No.6. N.W. Corner of wood ¼ S.W. of ¼ in. MONTAGNE. DE BLIGNY. 1 platoon in support on BLIGNY–CHAMBRECY road west of point 181.8.   1 platoon in Reserve in copse due south of point 181.8. |

WAR DIARY or INTELLIGENCE
Summary

Place	Date	Hour	Summary of Events and information
Line	6/6/18	-	A protective patrol of 1 Officer and 50 OR patrolled nightly along the track running North & South, on the east side of MICHEL HENUUT Farm. On the night of the 5th & 6th June a 6th the posts Nos.1 to 4 inclusive were taken over by the 9th CHESHIRES, and the 9th WELCH Line between the woods on the western slope of the MONTAGNE DE BLIGNY was thickened by 4 posts. The L.G. post and 1 Rifle post was also dug in in the wood nearest the road.
"	8/6/18	-	At 3.0 am. on the 8th of June the enemy fired down on the BLIGNY-CHAMBRECY road and on the crest of the hill. This barrage Lasted 1¼ hrs and then the enemy infantry attacked the WELCH Line from the direction of MICHEL HENUUT Farm. The attack was repulsed and three times he was driven back bayou. L.gun and Rifle fire. His Losses were very heavy among the troops attacking and also among some reserves which were formed up on the CHAMBRECY-SARCY road. At 10. a.m. the enemy delivered a strong attack in the direction of BLIGNY and at the same time he commenced shelling the 9th WELCH posts causing considerable casualties. At 11.30 noon it was found necessary to reinforce the posts and accordingly an officer and two sections from the support platoon went out to the posts. At 1.0 pm. the 9th Cheshires on the right withdrew to the BLIGNY-CHAMBRECY road. The enemy thereupon advanced to the crest of the MONTAGNE DE BLIGNY and commenced to dig himself in without opposition. He also entered the wood S.W. of the M. in MONTAGNE DE BLIGNY occupying all the posts which had been held over by the 9th Cheshires by the 9th WELCH the previous night. In consequence the right flank or post of the 9th Welch was seriously menaced and the whole Line of the 9th Welch and 9.R.W.F. was in danger of being surrounded and cut off. The remainder of the support platoon was then ordered for counter-attack, and endeavour to regain the wood and secure the position on the right flank of the 9th Welch. They attacked three times but each time repulsed by heaves machine gun fire from the CHAMBRECY-SARCY road. At 5.0 pm. The 9th Cheshires counter-attacked and retook the crest of the hill, but the wood on the western slope was still in the hands of the enemy who was holding it with about eighty men. The remaining 9th Welch reserves then attempted to retake the wood. They made 3 counter-attacks with covering Machine gunfire, but were unable to obtain a foothold in the wood owing to heavy casualties caused by hostile shelling and machine guns. At the time of relief 1.0 am. the enemy was still holding the four posts of the 9th Cheshires in the wood and efforts to retake same had cost the 9th Welch 2 Officers and 50. O.R. as casualties and 9th R.W.F. One Officer and 15 O.R.. Marched to BOIS DE Courton near Nautuil. Remained at BOIS DE Courton from the 8th to 11th June. On the night of the 11th the Battalion moved to support Line about 500 yds. in front of Chaunuys (on the Left). Situation fairly quiet, casual shelling. Remained in support until relieved by the Italians on the morning of the 19th, 2.0 am. June. Marched back to BOIS DE Courton. Then each Company proceeded to join the personel Left out of the Line. The 9th Welch marched to wood near Hautvillers. Casualties for this time in the Line: 13 officers and 477. Other Ranks
	8/6/18 to 19/6/18		

WAR DIARY or INTELLIGENCE
SUMMARY

Place	Date	Time	Summary of Events or information
Hautvillers	20/6/18	6 A.m	The Battalion marched to Cramant (passing through EPERNAY and was joined by the Transport near St Pierry) Reaching Cramant. Noon.
Cramant	21/6/18	7 A.m	Embussed and journeyed to Broussy-Le-Grand
Broussy-Le-Grand	22/6/18		Draft of 1 Officer. (Capt. H.M. Sulman M.C.) and 273 other Ranks.
"	23/6/18		Re-organisation of Battalion.
"	24/6/18		Training and firing on Range. Draft of 27 Other Ranks, mostly Casuals.
"	25/6/18		"
"	26/6/18		"
"	27/6/18		Draft of 5 Officers (2nd Lt H.C. Williamson. 2nd Lt H.R. Evans. 2nd Lt W.E. Hodgins. 2nd Lt A.J. Bradley. 2nd Lt J. Jeffery.
"	28/6/18		Training.
"	29/6/18		"
"	30/6/18		The Battalion with Transport proceeded by march route. Starting at 4.30 a.m. to Vassement. Arriving there about 6 p.m.

A.B. Jones Lt Colonel
Comdg 9th (S) Bn The Welch Regiment.

9

9 Welsh Army Form C. 2118.

Vol 35

WAR DIARY
or
INTELLIGENCE SUMMARY.
(Erase heading not required.)

Instructions regarding War Diaries and Intelligence Summaries are contained in F. S. Regs., Part II. and the Staff Manual respectively. Title pages will be prepared in manuscript.

Place	Date	Hour	Summary of Events and Information	Remarks and references to Appendices
Vassemont	1-7-18		The Battalion marched to Sommesous to entrain to New Area.	
Sommesous	2-7-18	12.18 am	Entrained for New Area.	
Anvin	3-7-18		Detrained and marched to Coupelle-Veille.	
Coupelle Veille	4-7-18		Proceeded by March Route to Ledinghem.	
Ledinghem	5-7-18		Parades. Inspection of Arms and Equipment. Training Programme prepared.	
"	6-7-18		" as per Training Programme. Draft arrived of 2 Officers { and Lt J.E. Williams } & F.E. Williams } and 195 Other Ranks	
"	7-7-18		Sunday. Church Parades.	
"	8-7-18		Parades as per Training Programme. Coys firing on Ranges.	
"	9-7-18		" " "	
"	10-7-18		" " Organization Parade	
"	11-7-18		The Battalion moved from Ledinghem at 3.15 to Enguinegatte Point and Embussed for Nowtheir arriving at Rely 7.30 pm	
Rely	12-7-18		Parade. Training Programme.	
"	13-7-18		The Battalion firing on large Range Auchy au Bois. Draft arrived consisting of 8 Officers viz:- 2nd Lt. Officer Runks Cpt Lewis Gardner Roll of Officers Lt A. Grant, Lt J. Pullar, Lt. T.H. Johns, 2nd Lt. R.S.L. Vaughan, 2nd Lt C.R. Froom, 2nd Lt. W. Shea and 2nd Lt R.D. Jenkins	mci
"	14-7-18		Sunday. Church Parades. Allotment of Baths for the Battalion at Auchy au Bois.	
"	15-7-18		Parades re Training Programme. Classes commenced - Bombing, Signalling, Musketry and Stretcher Bearers	

(A9173) Wt. W.3355/P360 60,000 12/17 D. D. & L. Sch. 52a. Forms/C2118/13

WAR DIARY
or
INTELLIGENCE SUMMARY.
(Erase heading not required.)

Army Form C. 2118.

Place	Date	Hour	Summary of Events and Information	Remarks and references to Appendices
Rely	16-7-18		Classes & Parades re. Training Programme. Battalion inspected re. Box Respirators	
"	17-7-18		Battalion Sports.	
"	18-7-18		Classes & Parades re. Training Programme. New class commenced Anti Air Craft Lewis Gunners.	
"	19-7-18		The Battalion on Tactical Scheme. proceeded by Bus to Training Area	
"	20-7-18		Draft of 1 Officer & 20 O.R. 1/Lt D.J. Davies M.C. Lecture by Divisional Commander re. Discipline Parades & Retraining Programme	
"	21-7-17		Draft of 21 Other Ranks. Gas Respirator argument. Church Parades	
"	22-7-17		Classes and Parades as per Training Programme	
"	23-7-18		"	
"	24-7-18		The Battalion on Tactical Scheme. proceeded by Bus to Training Area Capt. D.K. Browne D.S.O. rejoined	
"	25-7-18		Classes and Parades as per Training Programme. Battn. at Muchy on Bois	
"	26-7-18		New class for training young N.C.Os commenced. Classes and Parades as per Training Programme	
"	27-7-18		Classes & Parades as per Training Programme	
"	28-7-18		"	
"	29-7-18		"	
"	30-7-18		"	
"	31-7-18		"	

R. H. Jones
Lieut Colonel
Commanding
9/th(S) Bn The WELCH REGT

WAR DIARY
or
INTELLIGENCE SUMMARY
(Erase heading not required.)

9 Welsh R.
Vol 36

Place	Date	Hour	Summary of Events and Information	Remarks and references to Appendices
Rely	August 1916 1st		Parades as per Training Programme	
"	2nd		"	
"	3rd		Church Parades. Special Voluntary Service for the Fourth Anniversary of the War	
"	4th		Parades as per Training Programme	
"	5th		"	
"	6th		The Battalion moved by bus to CHOCQUES, halt and lie prepared and the Company's hidden in the long corn until dusk when they moved to the SUPPORT LINE behind HINGES, Battalion H.Q. SUFFOLK HOUSE	
SUPPORT LINE	7th		Situation Normal	
"	8th		"	
"	9th		"	
"	10th		The Battalion relieved the 2nd WILT'S REGT in the front line. E.A. active. Slight gas shelling Battalion H.Q. HINGES	
Front Line	11th		Situation quiet	
"	12th		"	
"	13th		"	
"	14th		" Battalion relieved by 9th Bn R.W.FUS during night 14/15 " A, B, and C Companys proceeded to billets in CHOCQUES, D Coy in Shropshire Line W.15.d	

WAR DIARY
or
INTELLIGENCE SUMMARY.
(Erase heading not required.)

Army Form C. 2118.

Place	Date	Hour	Summary of Events and Information	Remarks and references to Appendices
Chocques	15th		Training as per Training Programme	
"	16th		" Reconnaissance carried out of the Quarry and precautions in case of attack. C.Coy relieved P.Coy in Shropshire Line	
"	17th		Canal Dock Localities. Church Parades. Baths allotted 16 P. Company	
"	18th		"The Foden Disinfector" was at duty. The Battalion relieved the 2nd Wilts Regt in Support during night 18/19. Dispositions of Coys as follows. Lt.R.Grant Rejoined Bn. A Coy 2 platoons Gordon Line and 2 platoons Canal Line B " Suffolk Line, C.Coy Left of Gordon Line, D.Coy Left of Canal Line.	
Support Line	19th		Situation quiet. Heavy enemy artillery active against Canal Line about 5.15 pm one E.A. flew low over our Line and was engaged by AA and M.G. fire.	
"	20th		" Hingette lightly shelled with 4.2 at 2.45 pm Casualties One Man died.	
"	21st		" No shelling. E.A. crossed Canal between Pont Hinges & Park Lane at 1000 ft was heavily engaged by L.G. and M.G. fire.	

WAR DIARY
or
INTELLIGENCE SUMMARY.
(Erase heading not required.)

Army Form C. 2118.

Place	Date	Hour	Summary of Events and Information	Remarks and references to Appendices
Support Line	22nd		Situation very quiet. 11b E.A. active. Casualties - one O.R. Cpl F.B. Saunders, 15 U.K. for transfer 1b R.A.F.	
"	23rd		Our artillery slow harrasing fire. The Battalion on night 23/24 relieved the 2nd Seaforth Highlanders in the Left Bde Sector of the Dul. Sector, and became the Outpost Battalion. Dispositions. A+D Coys 2 platoons each in outpost Line, remaing platoons in immediate support, B. C. Coys held the Support Line which ran along Linnet Road. Advanced Battalion H.Q established at Q.29.d.2,4 and rear B.H.Q at Q.34.a.8.2. Casualties Nil.	
F.Dul Line	24th		Line ran approximatly R.26.a.a.9, R.26.a.4.3, R.26.c.8.6, R.26.d.2.a, R.32.b.6.5. Shelled with H.E. in Battalion area and communication cut by shell. Aircraft of our own active and two hostile balloons fell in flames direction N.E. Light T.M. hostile shelling of our forward posts, another hostile balloon brought down in flames. Our patrols active during day and were fired on by M.G.	
"	25.		Between 4.30 am and 7.am considerably enemy shelling of Lane between Love and Lone Lane with H.E. also few gas shells and indiscrimate shelling of Coy posts. Two Large E.A. flew over our positions. Enemy T.M. caused trouble during night 24/25. approximate map reference R.26.D.55. Casualties 5 O.R.	

Army Form C. 2118.

WAR DIARY
or
INTELLIGENCE SUMMARY.
(Erase heading not required.)

Instructions regarding War Diaries and Intelligence Summaries are contained in F. S. Regs., Part II. and the Staff Manual respectively. Title pages will be prepared in manuscript.

Place	Date	Hour	Summary of Events and Information	Remarks and references to Appendices
Frontline	26th		Situation Normal. Two hostile aircraft crossed our overlines and hovered over the Division for ¾ hour. They were heavily engaged by our L.G. and riflemen. Several patrols went out during day, and located various enemy posts. Casualties S.O.R. Wounded.	
"	27th		Situation Normal. Towards night heavy enemy shelling. The Battalion was relieved by the 9th R.W.FUS. and the Battalion on relief when in new positions became the LEFT BATTALION in the BATTLE ZONE. BATTALION H.Q. in HALFWAY HOUSE. W.2.b.4.5. Casualties Omr.	
"	28th		Situation quiet. No enemy shelling	
"	29th		" "	No E.A. active
"	30th		" "	
"	31st		" "	

F Brotherton
Major
Comdg 13th Bn Royal Welsh R of R

To OC 4th Brigade 14
[illegible]

Herewith War Diary
for Month of September 1918.

[signature]
Capt/Col.
LIEUT. COLONEL
COMDG. 9TH (SER) Bn. THE WELCH REGT.

[stamp: ORDERLY ROOM - 6 OCT 1918 9th (Ser) Bn. THE WELCH REGT.]

9th (S.) Bn. Welsh Regt.

WAR DIARY
or
INTELLIGENCE SUMMARY.

9 Welsh Regt
Army Form C. 2118.
September 1918.

Vol 37

Place	Date	Hour	Summary of Events and Information	Remarks and references to Appendices
	1.		Battalion moved up from HALFWAY HOUSE W.2 b 55 to a support position in U.30 a,c,d & U.36 b & d. Dispositions of Coy's were as follows A Coy West of GLEBE STREET in U.30 c, B Coy to position E of WILLOT LINE in U.36 d, C Coy about U.30 b. D Coy in U.36 c. Battn. HQ. U.36 a. #.3.	Not A
	2.		The general line ALEX BAILLEUL – OXFORD ROAD – CROIX BAR BLÉ – RIE HITZ BOURG ST VAAST was to be attacked on Septr. 3rd. 58th Bde was to attack on right & 57th Bde. 2nd Welsh Regt. were to attack on left. Division on left Bde on right were (with Regt. on right) Bns. 5.9. Division, and were to attack on left on 2nd Welsh Regt. Bn. on right gas The Battn. moved up & assembled on a line from road Northern in R.30 b – and in R.36. A Coy on left (A. & G. Tones) C Coy in centre (Capt. J. H. L. Drummond) D Coy on right (H. Hallam) B Coy in reserve Battn. HQ (Capt N. Nicolson). The Battn. objective was	Not A 376 sheet 6 map

WAR DIARY
or
INTELLIGENCE SUMMARY.
(Erase heading not required.)

Army Form C. 2118.

Place	Date	Hour	Summary of Events and Information	Remarks and references to Appendices
	2.		Shown on Map. B.	
	3.		BN read hrs 5:30 am. the Battn advanced under our own artillery and M.G. barrage. Very little resistance was fatter encountered, the fire of the barrage 100× un 3" rounds was found to be given a rifle. The whole Map B. Bn however marched off to its left & completely found all objectives. The further line reached by the Battn is shown on Map. B. – the 2" & with Regt prepared with this line on our left. The approximate line was refused to the 10. Division which is served a withdrawal to the line of the LABASSEE road, therefore dug up a line as shown on Map B. This line was held on a 2 Coy frontage H Coy on left D Coy on right, C Coy in support W. y. etc at BASSEE ROAD B Coy about CROIX BARBEE. During night 3/4	

WAR DIARY
or
INTELLIGENCE SUMMARY.

Army Form C. 2118.

Place	Date	Hour	Summary of Events and Information	Remarks and references to Appendices
			Word was received that the 6th Bde were pushing forward & that their objective was a line (6b) British Support line). These patrols were to be followed by the remainder of the Coys & D Coy's orders were to on and reinforce this line including suddenly setting were then ordered to find fr— wards to the OLD BRITISH FRONT LINE. Resistance was met with on HORRA River, the line were however taken on during the afternoon of H4. Total casualties during 3 + 4 : 37 O.R. Honours awarded Senior Lt. Mr Evans C Coy Military Cross, 26814 Pte Gilbard DCM. 8969 Sgt H Williams MM 19652 L/Cpl Chapman MM. 54635 Pte T Tenner Bn inglen H/S the Battn was relieved by 8th Gloucs Regt moved back to LOCON.	

(A9175) Wt W2358/P360 60,000 12/17 D. D. & L. Sch. 5[?]a. Forms/C2118/13

WAR DIARY
or
INTELLIGENCE SUMMARY.

(Erase heading not required.)

Army Form C. 2118.

Instructions regarding War Diaries and Intelligence Summaries are contained in F. S. Regs., Part II. and the Staff Manual respectively. Title pages will be prepared in manuscript.

Place	Date	Hour	Summary of Events and Information	Remarks and references to Appendices
Locon	5th		The Battalion under canvas. Battalion H.Q and 1 coy at X.13.d.7.7.	1 coy at X.7.c.5.5 (West side of Locon Road) 1 coy " X.7.c.7.5 (East " " ") 1 coy " X.13.a.2.4 (East " " ")
"	6th		Training as per Programme.	
"			Divine Service commenced. Training as per Programme	
"	7th		Training as per Programme	
"	8th		Training as per Programme	
"	9th		"	
"	10th		The Battalion relieved the 8th Gloster's in the Left Sub-sector of Left Bde Sector during the night 10/11th Sept. Dispositions as follows: Picquet Line. Left Front. A Coy. Right " B " Outpost Line of } Left... C Resistance } Right... D Battalion H.Q. M.28.d.9.2.	

WAR DIARY
or
INTELLIGENCE SUMMARY.

(Erase heading not required.)

Army Form C. 21

Instructions regarding War Diaries and Intelligence Summaries are contained in F. S. Regs., Part II. and the Staff Manual respectively. Title pages will be prepared in manuscript.

Place	Date	Hour	Summary of Events and Information	Remarks and references to Appendices
Front Line	11th		Situation Quiet.	
"	12th		Slight shelling. Casualties 5 O.R. wounded.	
"	13th		Casualties 1 O.R. wounded. 2 gassed.	
"	14th		Situation Quiet. The Battalion relieved by the 2nd Bn. Wiltshire Regt during night 14/15th Sept	
Line of Retention	15th		On relief the Battalion moved into Bde Reserve about CROIX BARBEE. Battalion H.Q. R.36.c.5.6. Coys in the Line of Retention.	
"	16th		Casualties 1 O.R. wounded.	
"	17th		" " 1 O.R. "	
"	18th		" " 1 O.R. Killed.	
Front Line	19th		The Battalion relieved the 9th Bn R.W. Fusrs during night 18/19th Sept in the left Sub-sector. Casualties 1 wounded.	
"	20		Casualties 1 O.R. wounded.	
"	21		" Pte J Jeffries Killed. 2nd Lieut Robert Evans M.M. wounded. 1 O.R. Killed. 5 O.R. wounded. 1 O.R. missing.	
"	22		" 3 O.R. wounded.	
"	23		The Battalion relieved by the 8th Bn Staff Regt during night 22nd/23rd Sept on relief the Battalion moved to camp at Locon vacated by the 1/4 K.S.L.I. at Wr D.7.8.	
			Casualties 1 gassed.	

WAR DIARY
or
INTELLIGENCE SUMMARY.
(Erase heading not required.)

Army Form C. 2118.

Instructions regarding War Diaries and Intelligence Summaries are contained in F. S. Regs., Part II. and the Staff Manual respectively. Title pages will be prepared in manuscript.

Place	Date	Hour	Summary of Events and Information	Remarks and references to Appendices
Locon	23rd		Training as per programme	
"	24th		"	
"	25th		"	
"	26th		"	
"	27th		During night 27th/28th Sept the Battalion relieved the 10th/R WARWICKS and 1 Coy of 8th GLOSTER Regt in the Left Sub-sector, Right sector of the line. Ref. RICHEBOURG. SHEET 1/10000 - 36.S.E 1/20000	
Line	28th			
"	29th		Dispositions of Coys. A Coy three platoons S.11 & 15.10 - Junction of MITZI Trench and La BASSEE road S.11.6.60.85. One platoon about S.11.6. 0.0. S.11.6.10.15.	
			B Coy from junction of MITZI Trench and LA BASSEE Road - LA TOURELLE Cross-roads	
			C Coy three platoons in Trench System from THIENE B - POPES NOSE one platoon in SEVEN SISTERS.	
			D Coy (Taking over from Company of 8" (Glosters) One platoon PORT. ARTHUR Trench, one platoon B.Line. Two platoons GUARD TRENCH.	

WAR DIARY
or
INTELLIGENCE SUMMARY.
(Erase heading not required.)

Army Form C. 2118.

Place	Date	Hour	Summary of Events and Information	Remarks and references to Appendices
Line	30"	6m 30.	3/W the 5t? Bde building the left sector of the Division from attaches & captures the general line of the DITCH running through M.36c, a-b M.30.D. M.25.c. In conjunction with this attack the 9" with Regt and 9" RW Fus advanced their line from the Lt SHEET ROAD to the line of the DITCH in S.11.a-e is in turndeling of this line through S.17 to +3.18.c. B Cy on La Rigalle (Lts D B Jones + C) went with S.Lyll Harrison but A Cy NX on left met with none.	

//WAR DIARY
//INTELLIGENCE SUMMARY.
(Erase heading not required.)

Army Form C. 2118.

9th (Service) Bn The Welch Regt

October 1918

C347.

WAR DIARY
or
INTELLIGENCE SUMMARY.

Army Form C. 2118.

(Erase heading not required.)

Instructions regarding War Diaries and Intelligence Summaries are contained in F. S. Regs., Part II. and the Staff Manual respectively. Title pages will be prepared in manuscript.

Place	Date	Hour	Summary of Events and Information	Remarks and references to Appendices
	June			
	1st		On night 1/2 and 2/3 the 19th Division were relieved in the line by 7th Division. In the night 1/2 the 9th Welch Regt were relieved by 16th R. Sussex Regt. On relief the Battalion marched on to LE TOURET and were then conveyed by train to BURBURE. Training was carried out by thirds and the Battalion did not leave LE TOURET till 07.30 hours 2nd.	
PRESSY-	2nd		The Battalion marched from BURBURE to PRESSY-LES-	
LES-PERNES			PERNES	
	do		The Battalion stayed on PRESSY on 3rd and on 4th entrained on PERNES at 20.30 hours for III Army three Coy Arty and detraining on SAVLTY L'ARBRET at 07.30 hours 5th	
			On detraining marched to billets on BARLY where the	
BARLY	5th		Battalion stayed until 7th	
	7th		On the afternoon of 7th the Battalion embussed & proceeded by lorry to GRINCOURT where N were bundles	

WAR DIARY
or
INTELLIGENCE SUMMARY.

(Erase heading not required.)

Army Form C. 2118.

Place	Date	Hour	Summary of Events and Information	Remarks and references to Appendices
	7		in bivouacs enviroms [?] there in field south about midday.	
CANTING 8			Battalion moved out on orders to the outskirts of CANTING - again in twenties bivouacs - where it remained until 10".	
	10		On the afternoon of 10". the Battalion marches to the outskirts of EMBRAL - and spilt from billets At time 19". Division were reserve Division of XVII Corps. Enemy were retreating but were fighting fiercely stubbornly on trail.	Appendix !
CHENONCELT 2			The Battalion moved to CHENONCELT - billets were quite from him there - were a flame of fire in the captured villages. The Battalion stayed here til 16" and carried on training for an attack on a wider battalion frontage (training hampered by No H)	

WAR DIARY
or
INTELLIGENCE SUMMARY.
(Erase heading not required.)

Army Form C. 2118.

Place	Date	Hour	Summary of Events and Information	Remarks and references to Appendices
AILEUX	16		Moved to AILEUX and came closer up to the line.	
			A few HV Shells in the vicinity of the village last-cellur. Had been fair, up till this date - but was turned dull and wet.	
	18		On 18th the Battalion moved up to AVESNES-LES-HUBERT preparatory to moving up for an attack. 19th Division were relieving 24th Division on the line near HAUSSY.	Appendix 2
	19		On night of 19th the Battalion moved to a position astride 2y V&G and 9th VMG. The Battalion was in reserve to 2nd WILTS and 9th RW Fus. who were attack- ing on left of 5-7" Bde. The enemy shou[w]ed Machine Gun across the R. SELLE and when the attack was carried out on 02.00 hours on 20th very few of enemy were encountered. On night 19/20 it rained very heavily.	Map "E".
	20		On night 20th the Battalion relieved 2nd Wilts	

WAR DIARY or INTELLIGENCE SUMMARY

Army Form C. 2118.

Place	Date	Hour	Summary of Events and Information	Remarks and references to Appendices
	22		Regn was firing line – we other shel very heavy.	
			bt During the afternoon we saw naval recover the enf.	
		16:30	During the Battalion moved ad'vance	
			up the line to the SOMMINE-VENDEGIES Railway	
			This was done under a Barrage at t.B. Guys & Capt	
			J.H. Downes M.C. and 2nd Lt. D.B. James M.C. respectively finding	
			forward Observers were not present – T.G. fine being	
			from the BEETROOT FACTORY and STATION. Than some	
			by the 61st Division came and attended in from	
			of 19th Division Infantry to an attack the	
			neat day the Battn then moved back to AULNOY	
			where it remained training till 31st.	
			On 28th Lt. Col W.P. Jones DSO proceeded	
			to England on a month's leave and Major Hammond	
			DSO MC having returned the Battalion on 18th	
			took over command.	

SECRET.   Copy No. 2..

58th Infantry Brigade Order No.277.   Appendix 7

                                                    10th October, 1918.

1. From all information to hand the enemy is carrying out a
    retirement on a large scale. A vigorous pursuit has been ordered
    along the whole Army front.

2. The pursuit by the LVII Corps is to be carried out with the
    utmost determination. The hostile rearguards are to be attacked
    as soon as located. The one aim and object of all ranks should
    be to get at the enemy's main forces and bring them to battle.

3. Corps boundaries are as shown on map issued on 9.10.18.

4. At present the 19th Division is in support to the 24th Div.
    Group.

5. The strictest march discipline of all arms is to be enforced.
    Troops are to move off the roads to halt whenever possible.

6. In the event of the 19th Division being ordered to advance
    through the 24th Division and so become leading group the
    Advanced Guard to the Division will consist of :-

            58th Infantry Brigade.
            2nd N.Z. Bde. R.F.A.
            2 Machine Gun Coys.
            94th Field Coy. R.E.
            Divl. Mounted Detachment.

7. In this event the Vanguard will probably consist of the
    following troops, the whole under the command of the O.C.
    Battalion:-
            1 Battalion.
            1 Sec. T.M.B.
            2 Sec. R.F.A.
            1 M.G. Coy.
            1 Sec. 94th Field Coy. R.E.
            Divl. Mounted Detachment (less 1 section).

    Every Battalion Commander will consider the handling of this
    force. Attention is directed to the diagram "An Infantry Brigade
    acting as an Advanced Guard" which shows a suggested formation
    for the Vanguard advancing when not in close touch with the
    enemy.

8. The Vanguard must act with the greatest vigour and boldness.
    Its duty is to drive in weak forces of the enemy and so avoid
    delaying the Main Guard. When the enemy is met with in strength
    the Vanguard will force the enemy to disclose his dispositions
    and hold him to his ground while dispositions for attack are
    made by troops in rear.

9. If ordered to move in fighting order Troops will dump
    haversacks with surplus kit and greatcoats rolled in bundles.
    The Pack will be carried but containing only fighting kit and
    leather jerkin when issued.

10. ACKNOWLEDGE.
                                                          Captain
                                    Brigade Major 58th Infantry Bde.

Issued through Signals at 1030 hours.

Copy No. 1 9.R.W.F.   8. B.T.O.   15 C.R.E.
          2 9.Welch R.   9 B.I.O.   16 O.C. Div.Train.
          3 2.Wilts R.   10 B.D.O.   17 O.C. No.4 Coy.Train.
          4 58.T.M.B.   11 56.Inf.Bde.   18 19th M.G.Bn.
          5 G.O.C.   12 57 -do-   19 Bde.Q.M.S.
          6 Staff Capt.   13 19th Div.G   20) War Diary.
          7 Bde. Sig. Offr.   14 19th Div.Q.   21)
                                                 22 File.

OPERATION ORDERS No. 16.
BY LIEUT COL. H.L.JONES, D.S.O.
COMDG 9th (S) Bn THE WELCH REGIMENT.   19/10/18.

Ref Sheet
51A S.E. & 51A S.W.

1. 19th Division will take part in an attack to capture the river SELLE and the high ground East of that river.

2. 58th Brigade will attack on a two Battalion frontage – 9th R.W.Fus. on left 2nd Wilts Regt. on right and 9th Welch Regt. in Reserve.
57th Inf. Bde will attack on right of 58th Bde and 4th Division on Left.

3. 9th Welch Regt will move tonight to a position of readiness about V.8.d. and 14.b. to be in position by 2200 hours. The Battalion will be prepared to move across the river when ordered to the line of the road in P.34.d. and V.5.a.
Companies will parade at 1930 hours ready to move off. Order of March, D., C., B., A., H.Q.
Companies will be disposed on a two platoon frontage.

        C.Coy Right Front.   D.Coy left Front.
        A.Coy right support. B.Coy left support.

Platoons should not be in regular lines but disposed so as to gain the maximum cover from the lie of the ground.
One Officer per Company will go up to reconnoitre the area this afternoon and will meet Coys on their way up this evening.

4. The attack will be carried out under a creeping artillery and M.G. barrage.
18 pounder barrage will open at ZERO on the line of the Railway and will remain there until Zero plus 15 when it will creep forward at the rate of 100 yards in 4 minutes straightening out over the Rly and halting for 9 minutes on Protector 200 yards beyond it. It will then continue to move forward 100 yards in 4 minutes till it reaches Protector 200 yards beyond second objective, where it will rest till Zero plus 70. It will then move forward at the same rate to Protector beyond third objective where it will rest till Zero plus 127 minutes. It will then continue at the same rate till it reaches Protector of final objective where it will remain for 15 minutes when barrage fire will cease. Strong patrols will then push forward to Railway S. of SOMMAING to capture any guns that may be W. of the Railway. One Battery R.F.A. will be pushed across the SELLE as soon as Bridges are ready, and will close support the Infantry, especially for Anti-Tank defence.

5. In addition to M.G's detailed for the creeping barrage one Company will go forward with the Brigade as forward guns.

6. To assist in maintaining direction, one round of Thermite (which gives a big flame) will be fired at each lift of the barrage to mark the flank of each attacking Battalion.
As the barrage lifts on the Protective barrage over each objective to allow the Infantry to come on to it, a salvo of Thermite shells will be fired by the Artillery along the whole front.

7. Rifle Grenades (3 Greens) will be fired when Battalions reach the final objectives. A proportion of these will be issued to C & D.Coys. They will not be used unless the Battalion is pushed through either of the leading Battalions. In this case C.Coy will be Right Front Coy, D.Coy Left Front Coy, B.Coy Support and A.Coy Reserve.

(W)

8. The possibility of an enemy counter attack with Tanks must be borne in mind.

9. Visual signalling will probably be the best and most reliable means of communication and must be made full use of.

10. The Signalling Officer will send a watch round to All Coys at 1800 hours and 2300 hours. The Brigade Signalling Officer will synchronise watches at 1700 hours.

11. Secrecy regarding the above operations is essential. Information given regarding them to troops should be the minimum compatible with the carrying out of their task.

12. Zero hour will be notified later.

    ACKNOWLEDGE.

                                                     Capt. & Adjt.
                                              9th Bn The Welch Regt.

Copies to :-
      C.O.   Adjt.
      A.   B.
      C.   D.
      T.O.   HQ.Mess.
      File.

WAR DIARY
~~INTELLIGENCE SUMMARY~~
(Erase heading not required.)

Army Form C. 2118.

Vol 39

9TH (S) BN. THE WELCH REGIMENT

NOVEMBER
1918

R. B. Jones
LIEUT COLONEL
COMDG. 9TH (S) BN. THE WELCH REGT

WAR DIARY
or
INTELLIGENCE SUMMARY.
(Erase heading not required.)

Army Form C. 2118.

Instructions regarding War Diaries and Intelligence Summaries are contained in F. S. Regs., Part II. and the Staff Manual respectively. Title pages will be prepared in manuscript.

Place	Date	Hour	Summary of Events and Information	Remarks and references to Appendices
RIEUX	1st		The Battalion was billeted in RIEUX.	
HAUSSY	2nd		The Battalion moved up to HAUSSY marching across country during the morning into billets in the BREWERY. At 17.00 hours it moved off again & marched out to VENDEGIES preparatory to assembling for an attack the following day.	
VENDEGIES				
	3rd		The Battalion moved up at 17.30 hours & assembled near PRESEAU. On arriving at B.P. JHC on ARMES on the way up to the Assembly Position - this is Map H. Commanding Officer was told that the enemy had fallen back then the Battalion would assemble on the JENLAIN - EVRGIES Road (see Map #). All Coys were therefore without warning from their original assembly positions the whole Battalion formed up on the HARLESEWES - ST HUBERT Road some 3 teams but the dt was a very foggy dy. 3/A- were 3 teams but the dt was a very foggy	Map H. Appendices # B. + D

WAR DIARY
or
INTELLIGENCE SUMMARY.
(Erase heading not required.)

Army Form C. 2118.

Place	Date	Hour	Summary of Events and Information	Remarks and references to Appendices
			For Day Major L. HAMILL DSO at was commanding the Battalion during from the operations. Company Commanders were as follows A. Coy Lieut G.G. Jones B. Coy Capt. H.V. Selwood C. Coy Capt G. Fitz-Simmons D. Coy Lieut E.H. Bayley. Casualties were - Officers wounded Capt G. Fitz-Simmons 2Lt H. Irvine 2Lt R.D. Price 2Lt L. Edwards 2Lt S.J. Davis. From B.H.Q. onwards the villages were all full of civilians who were very enthusiastic on the return of the British troops. The Battalion had no casualties on Nov. 9th. the enemy having retreated seventy miles. The weather was fine for the first and 2nd. being the finest days.	Appendices C. & F.
LERMINGHEN			The Battalion moves back to billets on HOUDAIN and	
near HULNOIS	11		rejoins the Depot and Transport. Moves on up to learn and marches to billet on WARGNIES-LE-GRAND, and were told on the way there	

WAR DIARY
or
INTELLIGENCE SUMMARY.
(Erase heading not required.)

Army Form C. 21?

Instructions regarding War Diaries and Intelligence Summaries are contained in F. S. Regs., Part II. and the Staff Manual respectively. Title pages will be prepared in manuscript.

Place	Date	Hour	Summary of Events and Information	Remarks and references to Appendices
			The Armistice had been signed and then hostilities ceased on 11th Novr	
	12.		XVII Corps HQ moved from WARGNIES and the Battalion moved into latter village	
	13.		The Battalion was employed on Salvage work near WARGNIES - fine weather	
	14		The Battalion moved to BERMERAIN - very cold and frosty.	
	15- 23		Moved to billets in AVESNES-LES-AUBERT. Schemes of education, recreation and demobilisation were published	
	24		The Battalion moved back to billets in CAMBRAI and remains there till 29".	
	29.		One hundred re-enlisted men transferred to Army Reserve Class W and were drafted to England via Etre Somme Dels. The Battalion moved by lorry to HALDY-LES- PERNOIS & of DOULLENS where	

WAR DIARY
or
INTELLIGENCE SUMMARY.
(Erase heading not required.)

Army Form C. 2118.

Place	Date	Hour	Summary of Events and Information	Remarks and references to Appendices
			Lt Col. H.J. Jones DSO rejoined and to took over command from Major Hammell DSO MC.	

Appendix A

At 0600 hours 4th November, 9th Welch Regt as Right Front Battalion of 58th Inf. Brigade attacked from the main JENLAIN - SUR GURGIES Road, the boundaries being L.11.c.8.0. - L.11.d.6.4. The first objective was the Spur in C.8.a & c. Battalion boundaries on this line being C.9.c.1.3. - C.9.b.9.9.

The assembly for the attack was rendered difficult as the enemy had retired on November 3rd from the area round ST HUBERT Cross Roads which was the original assembly position, and a new and un-reconnoitred line had to be taken up.

The Battalion attacked under a creeping barrage moving 100 yards every 5 minutes with 2 Companies in the front line, 1 in Support and 1 in Reserve. Direction was easy to maintain and the objective was reached with slight casualties. The PETIT AUNILLE River proved to be more of an obstacle than was anticipated. After reaching the GREEN LINE the barrage was originally timed to rest as a protector for 20 minutes but this was afterwards changed to 10 minutes. On the cessation of barrage fire, the Right front Company had been ordered to push out a liaison Post to G.9.d.0.0. to meet 56th Brigade on our Right and to advance its line to conform with this post. The two front Companies were also ordered to push forward strong patrols to BRY to ascertain if the high ground N.E. of that Village was held, and if not, to occupy it. 56th Brigade had however been temporarily been held up in WARGNIES-LE-GRAND so that the liaison Post was not established for an hour after the objective was reached. Within a quarter of an hour of the cessation of barrage fire, heavy machine gun and shell fire was opened on the ridge in C.8.a & c. which made the occupation of the ridge N.E. of BRY impossible without Artillery Support. Patrols managed to penetrate into ETH but were heavily fired upon.

An attack was therefore ordered to take place under a barrage at 1630 hours. Howies were to fire upon the high ground N.E. of BRY, but a smoke barrage could not be arranged. The objectives for this attack was the ROISIN - WARGNIES-LE-GRAND Road from G.10.a.9.7. to G.10.d.3.5. The 56th Brigade was to attack with its objective the line of this road S. of 9th Welch Regt. 2nd Wilts. Regt. were to attack on the left of 9th Welch with their right on the road and their left flank thrown back to occupy the Spur in A.28.

9th Welch Regt attacked with two fresh Companies in the front line, each Company having an extra Platoon attached in close support for mopping up purposes. The remaining two platoons of this Company were to take up a position N.E. of the River SART about G.10.c.8.8. and the Reserve Company was to take up a line about G.9.c.5.8. to command the exits to the Village and the crossings of the SART. As soon as the attack started a heavy barrage was put down on the ridge in C.8.a & c. which inflicted severe casualties on the reserve and support Companies. Heavy M.G. fire was also opened. The Right Company managed to gain its objective and gained touch with the 56th Brigade, but the 2nd Wilts Regt could not reach the Spur in A.28. and a defensive flank was therefore thrown back from LA HOULETTE to ETH along road G.10.a.0.9.

On the morning of 5th, the advance was continued and the line of the road through C.6.c. and 12.a. was reached without opposition. At this point the 9th R.W.Fusiliers pushed through the 9th Welch Regt. which was withdrawn into Brigade Reserve to BRY. The Battalion remained in BRY on 6th and moved to BETTREGHIES on 7th.

At BETTREGHIES on the afternoon of the 7th November, orders were received that the advance would be continued with the utmost energy and the 9th Welch Regt were to be attached to the 57th Inf. Brigade, who were to carry out the advance.

At 0500 hours on the 8th November the Battalion moved to BREAUGIES. The advance was being carried out on a two Battalion frontage - 10th R.Warwicks on left, 3rd Worcester Regt on Right, 9th Welch Regt left support, 8th Gloster Regt right support. The supporting Battalions were to keep approximately 2,500 yards behind front Battalions. Touch had been temporarily lost with the enemy. About 0845 hours, news was received that TAISNIERES had been occupied and the 9th Welch Regt. pushed forward via HOUDAIN and reached the BREWERY in I.4.c. where news came through that opposition had been encountered on the W. edge of the BOIS DE LANIERE. The 11th Division on the left of 57th Inf. Bde at this time (1200 hours) having just occupied HERGIES, heavy casualties were being inflicted on the 10th R.Warwicks from their left flank.

The 9th Welch Regt. therefore posted a Company as flank guard occupying the Spur in I.5.c & d. About 1700 this Company was relieved by 9th Cheshire Regt. which was moved up to form a flank from the 11th Division to the 57th Bde.

During the evening of November 8th, orders were received that the whole of the 57th Brigade with the 9th Welch Regt would attack at 0730 hours on November 9th and would capture the high ground N. of BOIS DE LANIERE and would also secure the Eastern end of the Wood. The 9th Welch had as its objective road and Railway junction J.4.b.0.3. - J.3.a.7.5. The attack was carried out with 3 Companies in the front line and one in reserve in MALPLAQUET. All objectives were captured on the Brigade front without opposition. The Battalion was then re-organised, having one Company on Spur in J.29.c., one Company holding the Railway J.4.b.0.3. - J.10.a.7.3., one Company round L'ERMITAGE and a reserve Company about J.3.a.1.0. About 1100 hours the 11th and 24th Divisions passed through the Battalion front and the whole Battalion was withdrawn to Billets.

APPENDIX "A"

ADMINISTRATIVE ORDERS
BY LIEUT COLONEL W. GODFREY. D.S.O.
COMDG 9th BATTN WELCH REGT.

1. RATIONS.
    14,000 Iron Rations are stored near the BRASSERIE.
    Application will be made to Brigade if rations fail on any day after "U" day.   days
    Every man will carry his Iron/Rations, Iron Rations, two days Oxo Ration and a tommy cooker to every two men.
    Water.
    Tanks and tins will be stored in front and new reserve line. These are not to be used on any account until "Z" day.
    On Z/A night water will be sent up on pack saddles.

2. AMMUNITION.
    Refilling point   N.1.c.4.2. (detonated here)
    Divisional bomb store   N.3. central.
    Brigade bomb store   N.11.b.2.5.
    Forward Brigade dumps at junction POPPY LANE & SUPPORT, N.12.c.8.5. and front line N.12.d.8.7.

3. MEDICAL.
    REGTL AID POSTS. N.12.b.2.5. STUART TRENCH   (left Battn)
                      N.11.a.5.7. POPPY.   (right Battn)
    Battle Aid Psts will be pushed forward after the attack.
    Regimental stretcher bearers will only carry to Regtl Aid Posts. Prisoners should be used.
    Advanced Dressing Station N.10.a.9.9.
    Main Dressing Station   WESTOUTRE.
    Walking wounded Collecting Post N.3.d.5.8.
    Walking wounded Main Dressing Station LA CLYTTE.

4. ROADS.
    Four tracks W, X, Y, Z, are being made from LA CLYTTE, - CANADA CORNER ROAD to VIERSTRAAT - KEMMEL ROAD.
    Three forward tracks to the front line are available from VIERSTRAAT - KEMMEL ROAD.
    Officers will copy these tracks on to their maps and have them reconnoitred.
    After the attack a forward track will be made and the VIERSTRAAT - WYTSCHAETE ROAD will be repaired.

5. PRISONERS OF WAR.
    (a) A Brigade Prisoners Cage will be established at N.11.a.7.5.
    (b) Prisoners will be sent back by Battalions capturing them to the Brigade Cage by cross country tracks. Escort should consist of slightly wounded men if possible and should not be stronger than 1 man to 10 prisoners.
    (c) After an escort has handed over its prisoners to the Officer i/c Prisoners Cage, the Officer will send such of the escort as are fit back to their units, ordering them to report on their way up POPPY LANE at the Main Brigade Bomb Store, N.11.b.2.5, where they will get their water bottles re-filled, and their S.A.A. replenished, and will be given bombs or other ammunition to carry forward to the line.. Slightly wounded men will be sent to the Walking Wounded Cllecting Station at N.3.d.5.8.
    (d) Officers and N.C.O. prisoners will be kept separate from their men and not allowed to converse with them.
    (e) Nothing will be taken from prisoners except arms and equipment. If, however, a prisoner is seen attempting to destroy papers etc., that he may have, they will be taken from him by the escort, who, will hand them over to the Officer i/c Brigade Cage or to the A.P.M.

6. STRAGGLERS POSTS.   N.6.a.1.2.
                        N.3.d.5.9.

7. VETERINARY SECTION.   at M.16.a.1.4.

(2)

8. R.E. STORES.
Main Brigade Dump N.11.b.1.4.
Advanced Dump at junction of POPPY LANE and Front Line.

9. SURPLUS PERSONNEL.
Camp N.4.c.5.0. Personnel to reach there on "W" day 6 p.m.
carrying rations for "X" day.
Camp will be rationed by Divisional Train.

10. TRANSPORT.
Two guides will report at Brigade Headquarters as soon after the objective has been gained as possible to guide pack mules with rations.
Transport Officer will call at Brigade Hd Qrs and if no guide is there, will act as ordered by Brigade and get into touch with his unit.

11. DRESS.
As per S.S. 135 para. XXX1, with the following amendments:-
Section 2, Sub-section V1. Delete Cap Comforter, Cardigan Jacket and Greatcoat.
Sub-section V11. Bombers will carry 120 rounds.
Rifle Grenadiers will carry 50 rounds.
Bombers will carry:-
Bayonet men   5 bombs.
N.C.O. & thrower 10 bombs.
Carrier   12 bombs.
Rifle Grenadiers 12 Rifle Grenades per man.
Section 1X. Flares issued will be divided equally between Companies.
Section X. 4 per man.
Section X1. As previously stated.
Section 4.
Sub-section 1   deleted.
"   "   111   75% of the men will carry tools in the ratio of 1 pick to 3 shovels.
"   "   V1   10 "P" Grenades per Company.
20 Smoke Grenades per Company.
4 "M.S.K." Grenades per Company.
The last are only to be used when no other means of clearing a dug-out is available.

12. SURPLUS KIT.
Government kit will be stored by Battalion arrangements.
Private kit surplus to that authorised will be stored at Divisional Stores, 198 Rue de la Gare, BAILLEUL on receipt of orders.
Officers will cut their kits down to regulation allowance.
Any kit in excess will be left behind.
Packs and Greatcoats will be left with the Quartermaster, by Companies.
Any private kit of N.C.Os or men will be stored separately by Companies in sandbags with name and number clearly marked and left at Quartermaster Stores.

13. SANITATION.
Latrines will be dug as soon as possible.
All sources of water must be carefully conserved and labelled by Units.

14. TROPHIES.
Captured War Material.
All articles claimed must be labelled and a claim submitted. If possible, number and mark should be stated.

OPERATION ORDERS (Continued)
BY LIEUT COLONEL E.GODFREY.
COMDG 9th BATTN WELCH REGT.

CONTACT PATROLS.

Aeroplanes for contact patrols will be R. E. 8 type and will be specially marked by a black flap attached to the rear of each lower plane.

Two contact aeroplanes will be in the air at the same time. One watching the area South of WYTSCHAETE and the other WYTSCHAETE and the area North of the Village.

Contact patrols will fly over the line and call for flares at the following hours, and any time subsequent to these hours at which special aeroplanes may be ordered :-

        Zero plus 0.45.
        Zero plus 2 hours.
        Zero plus 4.20.
        Zero plus 5.30.
        Zero plus 6.30.
        Zero plus 11 hours.

Troops will also be prepared to put out flares at any other time if the aeroplane calls for them.

Aeroplanes will call for flares and WATSON FANS by sounding a Klaxon Horn or firing a "VERY" white light, or both.

Green flares will be used. They should be lit in bunches of three each about 30 yards apart.

WATSON Fans will be used in conjunction with flares. The Fans should be turned over every two seconds and not quicker, that is, the white side will be exposed to the aeroplane for two seconds, then the dark side for two seconds, and so on.

In order to obtain as early intimation as possible from our own aeroplanes of hostile counter attacks, the following procedure will be adopted :-

"On the hostile infantry being seen to leave their trenches and advance, the Observer will send down by "wireless", "S.O.S." followed by the Zone call - no map co-ordinates will be given. This will constitute a request to our Artillery to put up a barrage on their "S.O.S." lines in that particular Zone.

A machine for this purpose will be up from Zero.
No aeroplanes will be in the air before Zero.

       58th Brigade Code Letter is L I .

The addition of W. X. Y. or Z. to the Brigade Code Letter will give the particular Battalion of the Brigade according to the "order of battle."

Z is the code letter for the 9th Welch Regt.

Synchronising of Watches.

From June 5th, watches will be synchronised from Brigade H.Q. at 8 a.m., 12 noon and 6 p.m. Telephones within 3000 yards of front line will not be used for this purpose.

CORRECTIONS.

   Para. 5. line 6. for "Zero plus 35 minutes" read "Zero plus 25 minutes", in Artillery formation.

   Para. 6. line 14. add "by Company nearest Strong Point."

OPERATION ORDERS.
BY LIEUT COLONEL W.GODFREY." D.S.O.
COMDG 9th BATTN WELCH REGIMENT.

Orders for the 9th Battn Welch Regt in amplification of Brigade Order No. 1654 already issued.

1. REFERENCE.
   WYTSCHAETE Sheet 1/10000 and Map X1.

2. BATTN FRONTAGE - BOUNDARIES.
   SUNKEN ROAD - N.18.a.7.8. to N.12.d.48.48.
   On BLUE LINE frontage of 275 yards.
   On GREEN LINE frontage of 230 yards.
   Right Boundary.
   N.18.b.23.53. - SUNKEN ROAD (exclusive) to O.13.c.32.88. -
   SOUTH CORNER, GRAND BOIS O.13.c.92.70. - OBVIOUS AVENUE
   (inclusive) - ESTAMINET CROSS ROADS O.20.a.30.87.
   Left Boundary.
   OBLIGE LANE - OBLIGE AVENUE (both exclusive) - O.13.b.25.13.
   on OBSTRUCTION SUPPORT - O.14.c.3.3. - South end of cutting
   O.14.c.

3. ASSEMBLY.
   The Wiltshire Regt on rght and R.W.Fusiliers on leftnin front line.
   Welch Regt on right and Cheshire Regt on left in Support Line and Borrow Ditch behind it.

4. BOUNDARIES FOR WELCH REGT.
   VIERSTRAAT - WYTSCHAETE ROAD (right) N.12.d.08.80. (left)

5. DISTRIBUTION - PLAN OF ATTACK.
   RED LINE.
   The Wiltshire Regt and R.W.Fusiliers will take the RED LINE.
   BLUE LINE AND GREEN LINE.
   The Welch Regt with the Cheshire Regt on their left and the 7th Royal Inniskillin Fusiliers on their right up to BLUE LINE and the 2nd Royal Irish on their right from BLUE to GREEN LINE will leave assembly positions to cross the British Front Line at Zero plus 35 minutes.
   The leading line will cross the RED LINE under her barrage at Zero plus 65 minutes and take the BLUE LINE.
   At Zero plus 3 hours 40 mintes cross the BLUE LINE and capture the GREEN LINE at Zero plus 4 hours 10 minutes.
   The Attack will be carried out in 4 waves, A.Coy on right, B.Coy on left, forming the first 2 waves with 2 platoons in eahh wave.
   C.Coy forming the third wave.
   D.Coy fomming the fourth. wave.

   All platoons when deployed will be in one line.
   C.Coy will be responsible for the flanks and will capture any strong point A and B.Coys have had to pass by.
   D.Coy will do all mopping up between the RED and the GREEN Line, exclusive of the BLUE and GREEN Line.
   Further orders are being issued to O.C. D.Coy.
   C.Coy will be prepared to assist D.Coy if that Coy is used up, and both C and D.Coys will be prepared to reinforce the front line if needed.
   As the frontage narrows, O.C. Companies must be prepared to shake out their waves into two lines if the wave becomes too thck.
   The advance through GRAND BOIS will be in sections in file
b with two scouts about 5 yards ahead.
   Specialattention must be paid to the barrage keeping up to the barrage and keeping touch.

(2)

...be 25 yards distance from the preceding line. C & D Coy
...increase this to 50 yards if Machine Gun fire becomes too
...strong, but the second wave must keep well up to the leading
...wave.

Direction.
O.C. A and B.Coys will each detail an Officer and N.C.O. to watch the direction of the right and left flank respectively.
Deployment will be made to the left.

Magnetic bearing of advance is 141 degrees.
Magnetic bearing of advance from OBVIOUS AVENUE is 101 degrees.

From the S.W. end of the RED LINE, A.Coy directing flank will make for the corner of the Wood.
From the junction of OBVIOUS AVENUE and OBVIOUS ALLEY, A.Coy directing flank will steer so as to leave NORTH HOUSE on their left.
During the advance, sections on each flank will dovetail with the neighbouring Battalion.
Dividing line between Companies is Nag Reserve and Tram Line inclusive to A.Coy to point O.13.a.55.25. - O.13.d.05.95. - O.14.c.00.25.

6. **CONSOLIDATION.**
BLUE and GREEN LINE will be consolidated, strong points in GREEN LINE being wired.
BLUE LINE. A new trench will be dug 100 yards to 150 yards beyond S.E. edge of the GRAND BOIS.
C.Coy will carry out this work but will move forward when the advance commences again.
GREEN LINE Consolidated as a line of Strong Points. R.E. will construct two strong points - O.14.c.3.3. - O.14.c.6.6. and C.Coy one at O.14.c.3.0.
C.Coy and those men not needed for fighting in A and B.Coys will improve the line.
Strong points will be joined up later.
When the R.E. have finished a strong point it will be occupied by 1 platoon with Lewis Gun.
A carrying party under 2nd Lieut. Harris will accompany Hd Qrs and will be pushed forward as soon as possible after the GREEN LINE has been captured.

7. **THINNING LINE.**
The 57th Brigade having taken the BLACK LINE, and D.Coy having finished mopping up, D.Coy will take over the GREEN LINE from A and B.Coys who will take up position in OBVIOUS ALLEY.
C.Coy will be in close support in trenches immediately behind the GREEN LINE.

8. **R.E.**
An overland track will be made forward to the GREEN LINE.

9. **MACHINE GUNS.**
There will be a creeping barrage in front of the Artillery barrage.
A sub-section (2 guns) will follow in rear in centre of Welch Regt and will take up position to sweep the ground between the BLUE and GREEN LINE.
It will advance in same position to GREEN LINE and take up position at about O.14.c.30.05.
As soon as the GREEN LINE is captured a second sub-section will come forward.
Guns will be under the orders of their own section commanders.

(3)

10. **STOKES MORTARS.**
    Two Mortars will be attached to the Battalion and will move in rear of the Battalion.
    Up to the BLUE LINE, one Gun will move along the line OBSTRUCTION LANE, one along OBSTRUCTION ALLEY.
    Up to the GREEN LINE, one Gun by OBVIOUS AVENUE and one Gun by OBSTRUCTION DRIVE.
    All Officers and N.C.Os must know the above positions, but as supply of ammunition is limited, and hard to renew, great care max must be taken not to call for a Gun unless absolutely necessary.

11. **ARTILLERY.**
    Creeping barrage.
    The barrage during the advance of the Welch Regt will lift uniformly 100 yards every 4 minutes.
    It will pile up on each objective on reaching it until the hour fixed for it to lift off.
    RED. Zero plus 35 minutes piling up for 15 minutes.
    BLUE. Zero plus 1 hour 40 minutes piling up for 27 minutes.
    GREEN. Zero plus 4 hours 10 minutes piling up for 2 minutes.
    Advance to start from:-
    RED LINE. Zero plus 65 minutes allows for 30 minutes in this line
    BLUE LINE. Zero plus 3 hours 40 minutes allows for 2 hours in this line.
    The 57th Brigade passes the GREEN LINE at Zero plus 4 hours 40 minutes allows for 30 minutes in this line before they arrive.
    Protective barrage, will lift off each objective 100 yards and remain for 4 minutes and a portion will then be employed on enemy's trenches.
    When the Infantry are due to advance, it will reform 150 yards in front of their line for 4 minutes, the last 2 minutes intense fire.
    The reforming of the barrage is the signal for the Infantry to move out.

12. **HEADQUARTERS.**
    Brigade   N.10.b.3.9.
    Wiltshire Regt   N.12.d.0.2.
    R.W.Fusiliers   N.12.c.9.6.
    Welch and Cheshire Regt NEW RESERVE N.11.b.9.2.

13. **COMMUNICATION.**
    Brigade forward station O.13.a.73.60 to proceed to O.13.b.3.2. after 57th Brigade pass GREEN LINE.
    R.W.Fusiliers, F.C.P. OBLIGE RESERVE O.13.a.35.80.
    Wiltshire Regt, F.C.P. NAG RESERVE N.18.b.98.48.
    Welch Regt.   F.C.P. about O.13.d.9.1. or in S.E. end of OBVIOUS AVENUE.
    Cheshire Regt, F.C.P. ONRAET FARM.
    Hd Qrs Welch Regt will move when the Battalion leaves its assembly position and take up temporary qurters at N.18.b.98.48. subsequent line of advance OBSTRUCTION LANE, OBVIOUS AVENUE. A F.C.P. will be formed at N.18.b.98.48. when the Wiltshire Regt move forward.

14. **S.O.S.** signal is made with Red Signal Cartridges as at present.

15. **ATTACK HELD UP.**
    If the Battalion on the right or left flank is held up, a defensive flank will be formed and the advance continued.

16. **TRENCHES.**
    POPPY LANE, BOIS CARRE and CHICORY LANE are "IN" trenches.
    STUART, P and O are "OUT" trenches.

ADMINISTRATIVE ORDERS (Continued)
BY LIEUT COLONEL W.GODFREY. D.S.O.
COMDG 9th BATTN WELCH REGT.

1. CORRECTIONS.
   Para. 1. WATER. for "Until Z day" read "Until Y/Z night".
   Para. 9. for "Camp N.4.c.5.0." read "Camp M.4.c.5.0."

2. WATER.
   Stored, Front Line N.12.d.8.7.
           Junction POPPY and SUPPORT N.12.c.7.4.
           New Reserve N.12.a.1.2.
   100 tins for the Battalion will be dumped in Support Line near junction with POPPY.
   No man is to use his water bottle before Zero hour.
   Water will be issued from the Tanks, and if necessary the tins during Y/Z night.

3. CARRYING PARTY.
   Advanced Brigade Dumps, Ammunition and R.E:-
       O.13.a.70.55. after capture RED LINE.
       O.14.c.1.7.   after capture GREEN LINE.
   Battalion carrying party under 2/Lieut. Harris will be 30 strong and will proceed in rear of D.Coy. They must be prepared to drop their stores and take part in the fight if the situation calls for it.
   If Brigade dump near RED or GREEN LINE is not formed, they must be prepared to get their second load from dumps further back.
   They will carry in the first advance:-
           192 Lewis Gun Drums.
           Screw Pickets & Wire (French & Barbed)
           200 Mills Rifle Granades.

4. RATIONS.
   Rum will be issued in the assembly trenches before Zero.

5. MEDICAL.
   Walking wounded go by X.1 and X tracks to N.11.a.5.7.
   Stretcher cases by STUART or X.2 track to WYTSCHAETE BEEK then north to N.12.b.2.5.

6. PRISONERS.
   Officers will be immediately deprived of all papers etc and these will be handed over to O.C. Cage with the owner.

SECRET.   OPERATION ORDERS No. 21.   Appendix
                         BY MAJOR L. HAMMILL. D.S.O. M.C.   B.
                      COMDG 9th (S) Bn THE WELCH REGIMENT.   2/11/18.

Ref. Map attached.

1. On 4th November 19th Division will attack and capture objectives shewn on attached map.
   The attack on the BLUE objective will be carried out by the 56th Bde. That on the GREEN & RED Objectives by 56th Bde on the Right and 58th Bde on the left. The 32nd Bde. of 11th Division will attack on the Left of 58th Bde.

2. Divisional and Brigade boundaries are shown on the attached map. Also the dividing lines between Battalions, and Companies of 9th Welch Regt.
   The Sunken Road in L.12.b. and G.7.d. is inclusive to 9th Welch Regt. The lines showing objectives are only diagrammatic. The tactical features in the neighbourhood will form the real objectives.
   Similarly, boundary lines are only intended as a guide to frontage. When necessary they may be crossed for tactical purposes.

3. ASSEMBLY.
   (1) The 58th Bde. will assemble on night 3rd/4th November. The 9th Welch Regt. will assemble in Square L.19.c. under cover of the Spur in that Square. The Reserve Battn of 56th Bde is assembling in Square L.25.a. and the Southern portion of L.19.c.
   (2) At Zero hour the 9th Welch Regt. and 2nd Wilts Regt. on left of 9th Welch Regt. will advance in rear of the Reserve Company of the Left Battn of 56th Bde. The leading Companies will keep in close touch by means of Officers, with the situation on front of the Left Battn of the 56th Bde. The 9th Welch Regt will form up for attack just behind the crest of the Hill marked 106.7 in Square L.16.a & b. and advance from this line so as to be formed up close under the Barrage forming the Protector to the BLUE Line in ample time to advance behind the barrage when it commences to move forward at Zero plus 155 minutes. It is of vital importance that Companies are ready to follow the barrage up to time, and if necessary they will push through the Reserve and Supporting Companies of the Left Battalion of the 56th Bde. during the advance in order to close up. The support and reserve Companies will follow at their normal distances. All ranks must clearly understand that the 56th Bde. are not advancing beyond the BLUE Line on the 58th Bde Sector, and they must push straight through them and form up under the barrage ready for its lift. Support Platoons will keep in close touch with front Platoons, and the Right Front Platoon of B.Coy. will keep very close touch with C.Coy. and will be prepared to mop up the SUNKEN Road on the Right flank of the Battalion.

4. The attack from the BLUE Line will be carried out by the 58th Bde. on a two Battalion frontage -

                  On Right   9th Welch Regt.
                  On Left   2nd Wilts Regt.
                  In Reserve   9th R.W. Fusiliers.

   The 9th Welch Regt will attack on a two Company frontage -

                  On Right   C.Coy.
                  On Left   D.Coy.
                  In Support   B.Coy.
                  In Reserve   A.Coy.

   Leading Companies will attack on a two Platoon frontage.
   Support and Reserve Companies will advance in Platoons in square formation until coming under fire.
   The total depth of the Battalion will be 1000 yards, and Companies and Platoons should be kept as compact as possible.

(2)

5. **ARTILLERY.** The attack will be covered by a creeping barrage of Field Artillery and Machine Guns. Up to the BLUE Line the barrage will advance 100 yards in four minutes. A pause of 15 minutes will be made on the Protector to the BLUE Line. The barrage will lift off this Protector at Zero plus 155 minutes. From the BLUE to the GREEN the rate of advance will be 100 yards in five minutes. On arrival at the GREEN a pause of half an hour will be made during which troops will re-organise and consolidate. Barrage fire will then cease and C.Company will push forward to the RED Line and will gain touch with 56th Brigade at L.P. G.9.c.9.1. A strong patrol will at the same time be pushed forward from both C & D.Coys to seize the River Crossings at BRY. If the situation permits these patrols will push forward to the high ground E. of BRY. and an Outpost line will be established on this high ground. C & D. Coys will report immediately to Battalion H.Q. if the latter can be effected. In order to assist in keeping direction, a round of smoke will be fired at each alternate lift of the barrage along the boundary of each attacking Battalion. As the barrage comes down on the Protector to each objective, a few rounds of Thermite will be fired along the whole Divisional Front.

6. **MACHINE GUNS.** One section of Machine Gunners will work in the Battalion Sector. Two Guns will be pushed forward as early as possible to the Spur in G.8.d. and 9.c. to cover the further advance of C.Coy. to the RED Line.

7. **CONSOLIDATION.** The GREEN and RED lines will be consolidated. C & D.Coys will consolidate in depth (if possible, two Platoons in front and one in Support) A & B.Coys will consolidate about G.8.a. & c. if C & D.Coys do not establish an Outpost Line E. of BRY. If this Outpost Line is established, B.Coy will hold and consolidate the RED & GREEN Line with A.Coy. in Support.
Rifle Grenade Signals showing three Greens will be issued to leading Coys. and will be fired on reaching the GREEN objective.

8. **SPECIAL INFORMATION.** Companies will forward as early as possible to Battalion H.Q. information as regards the kind of obstacle formed by the PETIT AUNELLE Stream and by the SART Streams when patrols reach it.

9. **HEADQUARTERS.** Battalion H.Q. will be in the vicinity of the Reserve Company and will move along the line of the SUNKEN Road on the Battn Right Boundary.

10. **CONTACT AEROPLANE.** A Contact Aeroplane will call for flares at –

    Zero plus two hours.
    Zero plus three hours.
    Zero plus four hours.

Front line troops will light flares (but will ensure that they are not all lit at the first call) and wave white flappers, maps etc.
A counter attack Aeroplane will be in the air from daylight onwards.

11. **WATCHES.** Watches will be synchronised at an hour to be notified later.

12. **SIGNALLING.** The Signalling Officer will make all necessary arrangements to enable Companies to keep communication with Battalion H.Q. by visual. Rear Battalion H.Q. will move by bounds along the line laid down as soon as the telephone is established with Brigade Forward Station from the forward bound

13. Zero hour will be notified later.

14. ACKNOWLEDGE.

    Copies to:- C.O.   Sig. Officer.
                ADJT.   T.O.
                A.   I.O.
                B.   C.
                D.   FILE (2Copies)

ISSUED AT... 0600 3/11/18

Capt. & Adjt.

9th Bn The Welch Regt.

"A" Form
MESSAGES AND SIGNALS.

Army Form C. 2121
(In pads of 100.)

Prefix......Code......m.	Words	Charge	This message is on a/c of :	Recd. at......m.
Office of Origin and Service Instructions	Sent			Date......
	At......m.		......Service.	From......
	To			
	By		(Signature of "Franking Officer")	By

TO— 11 Cps.

| Sender's Number. | Day of Month. | In reply to Number. | AAA |
| WS/60 | 8. | | |

1. The 6? Bde with 9 Welch Regt attached will carry out an attack tomorrow morning to form a defensive flank for 11th Division. The objective will be the high ground row from J.3.c.2.9 to J.5.a.7.9. The attack will be carried out by 4 Battns 10 H Warwicks on left, 9 Welch Regt & Gloster Regt, 3rd Worcest Regt on right.

2. The boundaries of 9 Welch Regt are junction of track and road J.3.d.3.9. J.2.a.3.6 — junction of road tramway (inclusive) J.4.b.0.3. The 8 Gloster Regt will attack on the right

From			
Place			
Time			

The above may be forwarded as now corrected. (Z)

....
Censor.   Signature of Addressor or person authorised to telegraph in his name

* This line should be erased if not required.

"A" Form
MESSAGES AND SIGNALS.

Army Form C. 2121
(In pads of 100.)

Prefix	Code	m	Words	Charge		This message is on a/c of:*		Recd. at m.
Office of Origin. and Service Instructions			Sent					Date
			At m.			Service		From
			To					
			By		(Signature of "Franking Officer")			By

TO {

| Sender's Number. | Day of Month. | In reply to Number. | AAA |

but will not assemble on the same line so that the right Coy will not form touch till the final object-ive is reached
3. The attack will be carried out on a three company frontage A Coy on right C Coy in centre D Coy on left B Coy in reserve
4. Position of assembly is the main ride of the wood from J 8 c 2.5 — J 3 d 1.0.
5. Route to assembly will be via foot-bridge J 10 c 5.0 near junction I 11 b 4.0 — J 8 c 4.9. A chain of runners

From			
Place			
Time			

The above may be forwarded as now corrected. (Z)

....
Censor. Signature of Addressor or person authorised to telegraph in his name
* This line should be erased if not required.

Order No. 1625. Wt. W3255/ P 511. 27/2 H. & K., Ltd. (E, 2634).

"A" Form
MESSAGES AND SIGNALS.

will stretch from Bn HQ
to extra foot bridge to
guide Coys

6. Order of march A. C. D. HQ
(B Coy will already be in
MTR PL(tre v T)) Coys will march
down by platoons at 100 yds
interval

7. A Coy will march at 06.30
fall Coys will be in position
by 07.00 hours

8. Coys will attack on a 2
platoon frontage & will consolidate in depth (2 platoons
in front and 2 in support)

9. There will be a 5 minute
barrage on the front ~~~~~~~~

MESSAGES AND SIGNALS.

Prefix...Code......m	Words	Charge.	This message is on a/c of:	Recd. at......m.
	Sent		......Service.	Date.........
Office of Origin and Service Instructions	At ......m.			From ....
	To			
	By	(Signature of "Franking Officer")	By.........

TO

Sender's Number.   Day of Month.   In reply to Number.   AAA

~~both~~ ~~will~~ ~~Start~~ a
won running through & J
2 central – J 36 0 1 – J H a O O.
This barrage will at last from
Zero to Zero + 5 mins. Coys
should therefore lie up
behind Jct Square to their
objective.

10 Zero hour is 07.30 hours.
11 Watches will be synchronised
by the Signalling Officer on
the way to assembly position
12 B.H.Q. during the attack
will be at J 10 a 9.8
ACKNOWLEDGE

From   A V 9 8
Place
Time
The above may be forwarded as now corrected. (Z)

Censor.   Signature of Addresser or person authorised to telegraph in his name
* This line should be erased if not required.

Order No. 1025. Wt. W3253/   P 511. 27/2   H. & K., Ltd. (E. 2634).

SECRET.   Copy No. 2...

58th Infy. Bde. Order No. 285.

Ref. Special map attached.

1. On 4th Novr. 19th Division will attack and capture objectives shown on attached map.
   The attack on BLUE objective will be carried out by 56th Bde. That on the GREEN and RED objectives by 56th Bde. on the Right and 58th Bde. on the Left. The 32nd Bde. of 11th Division will attack on the Left of 58th Bde.

2. The Divisional and Bde. Boundaries are shown on the attached map. Also the Dividing Line between Bns.
   The Sunken Road in L.12.b. and G.7.d. is inclusive to the Bde.
   The lines showing objectives are purely diagrammatic, the Tactical features in the neighbourhood form the real objectives.
   Similarly Boundary lines are only intended as a guide to frontages. They may always be crossed for tactical purposes when necessary.

ASSEMBLY & FORMING UP FOR ATTACK.

3. (a) The Brigade will assemble on night of 3rd/4th Novr. as follows :-

   Two leading Bns. in Squares L.19.c. and K.24.d. approximately as shown on map, under cover of the Spur in L.19.c. and a.
   Reserve Bn. in Square K.30.a. The Reserve Bn. of 56th Bde. is assembling in L.25.a. and the Southern portion of L.19.c.
   Assembly positions are to be carefully reconnoitred on morning of 3rd Novr. and positions marked if necessary. Positions selected for Bn.H.Q. to be reported as soon as possible.
   The 2 Forward Sections of Machine Guns and the L.T.M.B. will select suitable assembly positions on morning of 3rd Novr. and report locations to Bde.H.Q.

   (b) At Zero hour the two leading Bns. will advance in rear of the Reserve Coy. of the Left Bn. of 56th Bde. They will, by means of Officers, keep in the closest touch with the situation on front of Left Bn. of 56th Bde. They will form for attack just behind the crest of the Hill marked 106.7 in Square L.16.a. and b. and advance from this Line so as to be formed up close under the barrage forming the protector to the BLUE Line in ample time to advance behind the barrage when it commences to move forward at Zero plus 135 minutes. It is of vital importance that Bns. are in position to follow the barrage up to time and if necessary they will push through the Reserve and Supporting Coys. of the Left Bn. of 56th Bde. during the advance in order to close up. All ranks must understand that 56th Bde. are not advancing beyond the BLUE Line in our Sector and they must push straight through them and form up under the barrage ready for it to lift.

   (c) Reserve Bn will follow the two leading Bns. at approximately 1000 yards distance as far as the hill in L.16.a. and b. and will be prepared to move forward from there as ordered. This Bn. will also be prepared, if ordered, to pass through the two leading Bns. on the GREEN Line and establish itself on the high ground East of the villages ETH and BRY.

4. The attack from the BLUE Line will be carried out by 2 Bns. in front and one in Reserve.

   On Right.   9th Bn Welch Regt.
   On Left.   2nd Bn Wiltshire Regiment.
   In Reserve.   9th Bn R.W.Fusiliers.

   The Right Bn. will attack on a two Coy. front with one Coy. in Support and one in Reserve.
   The Left Bn. will advance from the BLUE Line on a one Coy. front pushing up a second Coy. on its Left as soon as there is room, and, if necessary, a 3rd Coy. to extend the Left flank

up with the right of 32nd Brigade at G.2.a.0.5 where a liaison post will be established. During the advance the Coys. echeloned on the Left flank will be specially on the look out for a possible counter-attack in a Southerly direction down the PETIT AUNELLE River Valley. The Reserve Company will eventually establish itself in a selected position about L.12.a. and G.7.b. with the special object of guarding this Valley.

The Reserve Bn. will move as indicated in para. 3 (c).

Liaison Posts shown on the map will be established by Bns. concerned from the BLUE Line onwards. 2nd Bn WILTSHIRE Regt. will have a party told off to take over the L.P. at L.11.c.2.7. from 56th Bde. as soon as possible after BLUE Line is reached. This party should be sent forward from Reserve Coy.

ARTILLERY ARRANGEMENTS 5. The Attack will be covered by a Creeping Barrage of Field Artillery and Machine Guns. Up to the BLUE objective the barrage will advance at the rate of 100 yards in 4 minutes. A pause of about 15 minutes will be made on the protector to the BLUE Line. The Barrage will lift off this protector at Zero plus 135 minutes. From the BLUE to the GREEN Objective the rate of advance will be 100 yards in 5 minutes.

On arrival at the GREEN Objective a pause of half an hour will be made during which troops will re-organise and consolidate. Barrage fire will then cease and the Right Bn. will push forward its line to the RED Line. Strong patrols will at the same time be pushed forward to seize the River crossings at BRY (Right Bn) and ETH (Left Bn). If the situation admits patrols will be pushed on the high ground East of these two villages and an Outpost Line established on this high ground.

In order to assist in keeping distance a round of Thermite shell will be fired at each alternative lift of the barrage (and 200 yds. beyond the latter) along the boundary of each attacking Bn. up to the BLUE Objective. From the BLUE to the GREEN Objective Smoke will be substituted for Thermite. As the barrage comes down on the Protector to each objective a few rounds of Thermite will be fired along the whole Divl. front.

MACHINE GUNS. 6. 2 Sections are allotted to the Bde. as forward guns. One Section will work in each Bn. sector. Their object will be to cover the advance of the attacking infantry by direct fire wherever this is possible. In the Right Sector two guns will be pushed forward as early as possible to the Spur in G.8.d. and 9.c. to cover the further advance on to the RED Line. In the Left Sector the guns will be disposed with special regard to the protection of the left flank and for defence against a counter-attack up the valley of the PETIT AUNELLE River. When this flank is secure guns may be moved forward to cover the advance of patrols towards the River crossings at ETH and BRY.

LIGHT TRENCH MORTARS. 7. 2 Mortars on Pack as long as possible will follow advance of leading Bns. They will be prepared to deal with opposition from Sunken Roads about L.11.d. and will eventually take up positions 1 to cover Sunken Road in G.9.d. and c. and one to cover Sunken Road in G.2.a. and the valley of the PETIT AUNELLE.

2 Mortars with extra ammunition will be in Reserve on Limber.

CONSOLIDATION. 8. The GREEN and RED Line will be consolidated. Leading Coys. will consolidate in depth. Reserve Coy. or Coys. of Right Bn will be about the Line of the Road in G.8.a. and c.

Reserve Coy. of Left Bn. will be disposed for defence of the valley of the PETIT AUNELLE.

Battalion Commanders will arrange the consolidation on the ground.

Rifle Grenade Signals showing three Greens will be fired by leading Coys. on reaching the GREEN Objective.

R. E. 9. One section of R.E. is allotted to the Bde. and will be employed for construction of Adv. Bde. H.Q. for the Bde. and Artillery Group.

- 3 -

SPECIAL INFORMATION. 10. Leading Bns. will obtain and forward to Bde.H.Q. as early as possible information as to the nature of the obstacle formed by the PETIT AUNELLE River and later by the SART Stream if patrols succeed in reaching it.

HEADQUARTERS. 11. Position of Bde.H.Q. at Zero will be notified later.
Bde. Forward Station will be at K.30.b.8.2. moving forward to vicinity of ST. HUBERT and later to about L.16.central.
When GREEN Objective is captured Bde. Forward Station will be established in Sunken Road in G.8.a.
On capture of BLUE Objective Bde. H.Q. will move to vicinity of ST. HUBERT.

CONTACT AEROPLANE. 12. A Contact Aeroplane will call for flares at -

Zero plus 2 hours.
Zero plus 3 hours.
Zero plus 4 hours.

Front line troops will light flares, wave white flappers, etc.
A Counter-attack aeroplane will be in the air from daylight onwards.

WATCHES. 13. Will be synchronised at an hour to be notified later.

14. Zero hour will be notified later.

ACKNOWLEDGE.

Captain

Brigade Major 58th Infantry Brigade.

Issued through Sigs. at 16.00 hours on 2nd Novr. 1918.

Copy No.			
1	9.R.O.Fusrs.	15	32nd Inf. Bde.
2	9.Welch R.	16	Left Group R.F.A.
3	2.Wilts Regt.	17	D.A.P.E.
4	58.T.M.B.	18	No.4 Coy. Train.
5	G.O.C.	19	94th Field Coy. R.E.
6	Staff Capt.	20	58th Fld. Amb.
7	B.T.O.	21	C.R.E.
8	B.I.O.	22	C.R.A.
9	B.B.O.	23	A.D.M.S.
10	Bde. Sig. Offr.	24	19th Bn M.G.C.
11	19th Div. 'G'	25	19th Div Tradn.
12	19th Div. 'Q'	26	War Diary.
13	56th Inf. Bde.	27	
14	57th Inf. Bde.	28	File.

SECRET.

Addendum No. 2 to 58th Bde. Order No. 285.

MACHINE GUNS.
1. "B" Coy. 19th Bn M.G.C. will co-operate with the Bde, 2 sections will act as forward guns.
   Remaining 2 sections under O.C. 'B' Coy will move forward at Zero behind the Reserve Battalion to the high ground about L.16.b.3.2. with a view to covering the advance of the Bde. from the BLUE Line.
   When the GREEN Line has been captured these guns will move forward to the high ground in L.12.c.

2. After capture of the RED Line O.C. 'B' Coy. will co-ordinate the consolidation in depth of all 16 guns.
   O.C. 'B' Coy will make his H.Q. with the Right attacking Bn (9th Bn Welch Regt) and will detail a Liaison Officer to work with the Left Attacking Bn (2nd Bn Wiltshire Regt).
   Thus either Bn. Commander may have the use of a proportion or of all the rear guns on application to the Coy. Commander or Liaison Officer as the case may be.

R.E.
3. 1 Section of the 94th Field Coy. R.E. will be allotted to the Bde. to extemporise bridges across the AUNELLE River. If possible bridges to take Pack animals will be extemporised at G.7.b.35.10. and G.7.b.5.6. approx.
   The Officer i/c Section will keep in close touch with the O's.C. the Attacking Bns.

Captain
Brigade Major 58th Infantry Brigade.

3.11.18.

Issued to 9/R.W.Fusrs.
9/Welch Regt.
2/Wilts Regt.
58/T.M.Bty.
19th Bn M.G.C.
94/Field Co.R.E.

WAR DIARY
or
INTELLIGENCE SUMMARY.

Army Form C. 2118.

9th (S) Bn The Welch Regt

FEBRUARY 1919

WAR DIARY or INTELLIGENCE SUMMARY

Army Form C. 2118.

Place	Date	Hour	Summary of Events and Information	Remarks and references to Appendices
BERTEAU-COURT	22		Presentation of Colours by Major-Gen. G.D. Jeffreys CB CMG Comdg. 19th Division. 2Lt. Hodgers Demobilised	
	25		2Lt T.T. Howe Transfent Officer and 15 OR Demobilised	
	26		13 OR Demobilised - due weather suddenly turned very cold and continues the same til the end of the month with occasional snowstorms. Lt. Col. H. Ll. Jones DSO left the Battalion for over with the PARIS Leave - Major P.H. Bradbury MC taking command.	
	27		Capt. E.W.S. Gardner MC and 13 OR Demobilised	
	28		2Lt. J.T. Rawlins MC MM and 14 OR Demobilised. From this date the Battalion was organised in two Groups A Group and B Group - A Group under the command of Capt. H.N. Salmon MC and B. Group under the command of Capt. D.R. Jones MC. The return strength on this June was about 380.	

WAR DIARY
or
INTELLIGENCE SUMMARY.
(Erase heading not required.)

Army Form C. 2118.

Place	Date	Hour	Summary of Events and Information	Remarks and references to Appendices
BERTEAU- COURT	1-3		Training continues - Start of football league (in Brigade) in afternoon.	
	3		Four men demobilised	
	4-10		Visited eight - the men were frendidly visited and "billed" and accommodated in a Nissen hut camp which was being erected under the supervision of the R.E. at the E. end of BERTEAUCOURT	
	12		Lieut Bayley and 9 O R demobilised	
	13		2/Lt O. Jenkins and 16 OR demobilised	
	14		2 O R demobilised	
	15		Lieut G.G. Jones demobilised - all the time the 9 Welch Regt and 9" R.W. Fus were tracking the renowned for the presentation of colours to take place on 22" Jan.	
	18-31/1		On these days 7, 11, 38 and 13 OR were demobilised respectively	

Army Form C. 2118.

WAR DIARY
or
INTELLIGENCE SUMMARY.
(Erase heading not required.)

9TH (S) BN THE WELCH REGIMENT

JANUARY 1919.

Vol 41

K. V. Jones, LIEUT. COLONEL.
9th (Ser) Bn. THE WELCH REGT.

ORDERLY ROOM — 4 FEB. 1919 — 9th (Ser) Bn. THE WELCH REGT.

41.6.
3 sheet

WAR DIARY
or
INTELLIGENCE SUMMARY.
(Erase heading not required.)

Army Form C. 2118.

Instructions regarding War Diaries and Intelligence
Summaries are contained in F. S. Regs., Part II.
and the Staff Manual respectively. Title pages
will be prepared in manuscript.

Place	Date	Hour	Summary of Events and Information	Remarks and references to Appendices
BERTEAUCOURT	20.		18 Miners were despatched to CAMBRAI for transfer to Army Lys Class (N). The Battn. foot-ball team played the final match for the Brigade Championship. The team of the Welshire Regt being the winners. Both Teams failed to register a goal.	
"	24/xs.		Education & training carried out according to Programme	
"	25.		Xmas Day celebrated by a Xmas Dinner, Church Parades were also carried out in the morning	
"	26/12.		Usual Routine. The following awards were also promulgated in Battn. Orders, Late A.M. Salmon MC. BAR to MC, 2/Lt J.G. Vaughan Charles MC, and Melville Williams.	
"	30.		— MC — 12890 CSM (A/RSM) Charles ME, and Melville Williams M1 Miners transferred to R.Res. Class (N)	
"			2/Lt DB RIBB. was the first officer to be demobilised being a "Purple Officer". One "Purple Man" was sent to Drocourt on the same day also	
"	31st.		— Usual Routine	

J.H. Bradbury Major
LIEUT. COLONEL
COMDG 9TH (SERV) BN. THE WELCH REGT.

WAR DIARY
INTELLIGENCE SUMMARY.
(Erase heading not required.)

Army Form C. 2118.

December 1918

Place	Date	Hour	Summary of Events and Information	Remarks and references to Appendices
HALLOY-LES-PERNOIS	1st		Training TStaff carried out under Company arrangements.	
	2nd		—do—	
	3/6/12		Usual routine. Lieut D.B. Jones M.C. and A/Capt —— commencing a Company.	
	7/12		Ballot Papers started to arrive. The men were given instruction as to how these were completed, but there seemed to be a lack of enthusiasm regarding a general election, the reason being that many had no knowledge of the prospective candidates.	
BERTEAUCOURT	11/12		Bn. Bn. before on the 11th to move to BERTEAUCOURT this being a much larger village than HALLOY and accommodation being much suitable. The Batn. were complete in the new billets by noon 12th and the fitting of Stoves & general improvements were commenced upon.	
	13/19		Training Education a Sports carried out according to their respective programmes.	GJB

Army Form C. 2118.

WAR DIARY
or
INTELLIGENCE SUMMARY.
(Erase heading not required.)

9th (S) Bn The Welch Regt.

DECEMBER

1918

SECRET

57th INFANTRY BRIGADE ORDER NO 259

Reference Map Sheet
51 1/40,000. 51 N.E. 1/20,000   November 8th 1918.

1. The 57th Infantry Brigade, in conjunction with Divisions on the Flanks, will continue the advance tomorrow morning, November 9th.

2. The 8th Glouc.Regt. will advance and occupy the spur running N.E. through J 12 A and J 6 D.
   The 9th Welch Regt. and 10th R.War.Regt will advance and form a defensive flank facing Northwards along the N. edge of the BOIS de la LANIERE, clearing out any enemy posts inside the Divisional Northern Boundary.
   The 3rd Worc.Regt will advance on the extreme right of the Brigade Front and occupy the Railway in J 17 A.

3. The approximate Objective Line, Boundaries and jumping off lines are shown on the attached Map.

4. The advance will be carried out without Artillery Support, except on the Front of the 9th Welch Regt and 10th R.War.Regt, where Artillery will fire as shown on the attached Map.
   Machine Guns will assist the Advance by engaging targets North of the Divisional Northern Boundary.

5. The 9th Welch Regt will be formed up on their jumping off line by Zero - 30, at which hour all troops of the 10th R.War Regt in J 3, and 4 C may be withdrawn.
   All troops of the 10th R.War.Regt in J 4 D and J 10 may be withdrawn when the 8th Glouc.Regt have passed through them.

6. The 24th Division is advancing at 0800 and the 11th Division at 0730.
   8th Glouc.Regt, 9th Welch Regt, and 10th R.War.Regt therefore will advance at 0730, and the 3rd Worc.Regt will advance at 0800.

7. Should GONGNIES - CHAUSSEE be found unoccupied by the enemy in the course of the day, the 8th Glouc.Regt will be prepared to occupy it.

8. Battn. Hd.Qrs. will be established as follows at 0730 :-
   3rd Worc.Regt)   J 14 C 7.9
   8th Glouc.Regt.)

   9th Welch Regt)   J 7 A 8.8.
   10th R.War.Regt)

9. Advanced Brigade Report Centre will open at J 7 C 4.4 at 0730.

H.W. Howe.
Major.
A/Brigade Major,
57th Infantry Brigade.

Brigade H.Q.

(2)

14. The 81st Field Company is to be concentrated in HOUDAIN by 1000 hours November the 8th for work in removing obstacles, and bridging.

15. COMMUNICATIONS.
All communication between Battalions and Brigade Headquarters will be by Mounted or Cyclist Orderly - or Runner.

16. BRIGADE HEADQUARTERS.
Brigade Headquarters will move in successive stages approximately along the inter-battalion Boundary, a Brigade Report Centre with telephone being established as quickly as possible along this line.
Advanced Brigade Report Centre will open at CHATEAU de WARNICAMP at Zero plus 30.

17. Zero hour will be 0600 hours, November 8th.

H.W. Howe
Major.
A/Brigade Major.
57th Infantry Brigade.

Brigade H.Q.

Copies to :-

19th Division "G"	6th Dragoon Guards.
19th Division "Q".	81st Field Coy.
56th Inf. Bde.	C.R.A.
58th Inf. Bde.	C.R.E.
72nd Inf. Bde.	A.D.M.S.
10th R.War.R. (5)	C.O.C.
8th Glouc.R. (5)	B.M.
3rd Worc.R. (5)	Staff Capt.
9th Welch R. (5)	Bde. T.O.
88th Bde. R.F.A. (5)	Bde. Sig. Off.
57th T.M.Bty.	Bde. I.O.
	Bde. Gas. Off.
	War Diary (2).

SECRET

57th INFANTRY BRIGADE ORDER NO.258.

Reference Map Sheet
51 1/40,000   7th November 1918.

Appendix E

1. The French have captured MEZIERES, thus cutting off the main German Railway S. of the ARDENNES.

2. If we pursue vigorously there is every opportunity of inflicting heavy losses on the Germans on our immediate Front, there being only one line (MAUBEUGE - NAMUR) whereby the enemy can feed his forces between the MEUSE and the SAMBRE.

3. The pursuit will be continued tomorrow, November 8th at Zero hour, and will be vigorously pushed forward regardless of fatigue or exposed left flank. Flank Divisions are continuing the pursuit at the same hour.

4. The Corps Cavalry are endeavouring to pass through the Infantry after Zero hour.

5. 57th Infantry Brigade, plus 9th Bn. Welsh Regt attached from the 58th Infantry Brigade, will carry out the advance.
Battalions will be disposed as follows :-
Right Front Battn.   3rd Worc.Regt.
Left Front Battn.   10th R.War.Regt.
Right Support Battn. 8th Glouc.Regt.
Left Support Battn.   9th Welch Regt.

6. Leading Battalions will advance on a two Company Front.

7. Support Battalions will follow leading Battalions, maintaining a distance of 2,000 to 2,500 yards from the rearmost formations of the leading Battalions. They will be prepared to pass through leading Battns. at any stage of the advance.

8. Brigade and Inter-Battalion Boundaries will be as already notified to Battalions.

9. The following will be successive bounds of the advance :-
   (a) Line I 10 Central - I 9 Central.
   (b) Line I 18 A - Crucifix in I 11 B - I 5 Central.
   (c) Line through Eastern edge of MALPLAQUET village.

10. These successive positions will be made good without a prearranged Artillery programme, unless the opposition is of such a nature as to require organised concentrations or barrage.
The advance of the 3rd Worc.Regt will be supported by A/Battery 88th Brigade R.F.A, and that of the 10th R.War.Regt by C/Battery 88th Brigade R.F.A. These batteries will act under the orders of Battalion Commanders. Battery Commanders will report to Battalion Commanders at Zero - 15.

11. Machine Guns will follow the advance in the formations already organised, the greatest possible use being made of wheeled and pack transport.

12. T.M.Battery.
The 57th T.M.Battery will follow in rear of the 10th R.War.Regt, making use of wheeled and pack transport.

13. "A" ECHELON TRANSPORT.
"A" Echelon Transport of supporting battalions will move with Battalions.
"A" Echelon Transport of leading Battalions will move under orders of the Staff Captain.

WAR DIARY
or
INTELLIGENCE SUMMARY.

Army Form C. 2118.

(Erase heading not required.)

Instructions regarding War Diaries and Intelligence Summaries are contained in F. S. Regs., Part II. and the Staff Manual respectively. Title pages will be prepared in manuscript.

Place	Date	Hour	Summary of Events and Information	Remarks and references to Appendices
BERTIE AU- QUATE	1st		Training under Company arrangements	
	2nd		Lt. Col. H. H. Jones returned from leave and <s>stationed</s> took over command of the Battalion. 2nd Lt. Bradley demobilised.	
	6		Major General J. D. Jeffreys left the Division to take over 30th Division. Brig Gen Glasgow took over command of 19th Division and Lt. Col. H.H. Jones took over 5.W. Inf. Bde. Major Bradbury proceeded on leave to Winchester. Capt. D.M. Bourne took command of the Battalion.	
	7		1 officer and 78 O.R. demobilised during 7th.	
	8		Orders received to furnish a draft of 5 officers and 100 O.R. to proceed to 6th South Wales Borderers, 30th Division	
	9		The Prince of Wales went through the Brigade area to see Battalion. Draft for 6th S.W.B furnished a separate Company	
	14		27 O.R. Demobilised during week.	

Army Form C. 2118.

WAR DIARY
or
INTELLIGENCE SUMMARY.
(Erase heading not required.)

Instructions regarding War Diaries and Intelligence Summaries are contained in F. S. Regs., Part II. and the Staff Manual respectively. Title pages will be prepared in manuscript.

Place	Date	Hour	Summary of Events and Information	Remarks and references to Appendices
BERTEAU	18		Capt L.H. Davies MC, Lieut T.H. Johns 2Lt HR Evans MC, 2Lt W.H. Griffiths, 2Lt J.G.L. Vaughan and 100 OR despatched to G.S.W. Bandeners.	
COURT	21		18 OR demobilies during week.	
	23		The Battalion moved by lorry to VILLERS L'HOPITAL where 57th and 58th Brigades were in E. Shell Camp.	
VILLERS	24		Orders received to prepare draft of 2 officers and all available retainable OR for 1/6 Welch Regt 12"	
L'HOPITAL			Division	
	28		7 OR demobilies during week. Ration strengths 115.	

D.H. Barnes
Capt. Comdg.
4th (S) Bn The Welch Regt.

Army Form C. 2118.

WAR DIARY
or
INTELLIGENCE SUMMARY.
(Erase heading not required.)

Vol 43

9th (S) Bn The Welch Regt

MARCH 1919

43.L.
3 sheets

Army Form C. 2118.

WAR DIARY
or
INTELLIGENCE SUMMARY.
(Erase heading not required.)

Instructions regarding War Diaries and Intelligence Summaries are contained in F. S. Regs., Part II. and the Staff Manual respectively. Title pages will be prepared in manuscript.

Place	Date	Hour	Summary of Events and Information	Remarks and references to Appendices
VILLERS L'HOPITAL	7.		2 OR Demobilised	
	13.		Draft of 2 officers (Lieuts. Pallan and 2Lt A.E. White) and 46 OR proceeded to join 1/6 Bn The Welch Regt in the Army of Occupation.	
	14		10 OR Demobilised	
	15.		Major P.H. Bradbury MC rejoined the Battalion from leave in England and took over command.	
	17.		Major Bradbury MC proceeded to England on two months furlough, having volunteered for service abroad with 2nd Bn N. Staff. Regt. Capt. D.H. Bonner took command.	
	19.		HQ 19th Division ceased to exist from night 18/19. March and the remnants of the 19th Division were administered by HQ 58th Inf Bde which moved to FROHEN-LE-GRAND.	
	20.		Lt Col H. Ll. Jones DSO rejoins the Battalion and took over command.	

WAR DIARY
or
INTELLIGENCE SUMMARY.

Army Form C. 2118.

Place	Date	Hour	Summary of Events and Information	Remarks and references to Appendices
VILLERS	27		2 Lts. Dixon, J.E. Williams, J.R. Davis and P.R. Heyes Demobilised and 5 OR	
L'HOPITAL	28		6 OR Demobilised	
	30		Cadre of 2nd Bn. Wells Regt. proceeded to England and the Surplus personnel of their Bn. were attached to 9 Welch Regt. (16 officers and 10 OR)	
	31		Ration Strength on 31st 76.	

Dunn N Bowne
Capt for Lt Col.
Comdg 9th (S) Bn. The Welch Regt

www.ingramcontent.com/pod-product-compliance
Lightning Source LLC
Chambersburg PA
CBHW082009220426

43670CB00014B/2583